The Power of AI and Algorithms

How They Shape Our Lives

by
Eleanor J. Carter

The Power of AI and Algorithms

How They Shape Our Lives

Contents

Introduction

In the frenetic rhythm of modern life, we're often caught in a dance with unseen partners—artificial intelligence and algorithms. They're omnipresent, influencing nearly every aspect of our day-to-day existence. Yet, despite their profound impact, these technological forces remain largely enigmatic to many. This book sets out to demystify AI and algorithms, illuminating the paths they've forged into our lives and their potential trajectories as we move forward.

Understanding AI isn't solely about comprehending complex computer codes or intricate data models. It's about recognizing the silent revolutions occurring in the backdrop of our routines—the predictive suggestions while you shop online, the automated texts that schedule your week, or the voice-activated assistants evolving into integral parts of our families. AI is making once-imagined futures a present-day reality, threading itself into the fabric of our social, economic, and personal tapestries.

The journey into the world of AI begins with unraveling its essence. Historically tethered to science fiction, AI has transitioned from the realm of imagination to that of factual presence. We've moved beyond merely envisioning mechanical sentinels to refining algorithms that subtly steer decision-making processes. The evolution from elementary computations to advanced algorithms reflects humanity's unrelenting quest to replicate, and perhaps surpass, its cognitive capabilities.

Yet, there's an irony to this advancement. For all its prowess, AI often remains shrouded in mystery. Many people use and interact with AI without recognizing its footprint. This isn't just a gap in understanding; it's an issue that affects decision-making, privacy, ethics, and future planning on a global scale. Our consciousness of AI's power—or lack thereof—shapes how we as individuals and societies adopt new technologies and draft policies to govern them.

It's essential to comprehend the dichotomy of AI—its power to do good juxtaposed with its potential to exacerbate existing vulnerabilities. AI can democratize learning and health care but might also deepen societal gaps. Algorithms can enhance our lives with personalized experiences but can also result in echo chambers that stifle diversity of thought. These dual-edged capabilities urge us to be both vigilant and optimistic.

The influence of AI extends beyond the individual, reaching into the realms of employment, social interactions, and ethical considerations. The workplace is transforming; roles are being redefined and efficiency optimized, all under the latent guidance of complex algorithms. The pace and nature of work are evolving, calling for a reassessment of skills and expectations. Similarly, AI's footprints in healthcare show promise in diagnostics and patient care, yet also require scrutiny regarding data privacy and ethical boundaries.

Moreover, AI reshapes societal narratives through its influence on media, creativity, and personal privacy. The stories we consume and the content we generate are increasingly filtered through algorithmic lenses. Understanding these dynamics is crucial, highlighting the need for media literacy in an age where digital manipulation can surge unchecked.

In exploring the ethical dimensions, we're compelled to ask: Who benefits from AI, and who does not? Are the decision-making algorithms fair and transparent, or do they perpetuate biases embedded in their training data? These are pressing questions as AI assumes roles traditionally governed by human judgment, from credit approvals to judicial decisions. Our ethical compass must align with the innovations we embrace, ensuring technology serves humanity equitably and justly.

Furthermore, while technology's promise lies in progress, it's equally vital to envisage the limitations of AI. Technical and philosophical boundaries define what AI can achieve today and in the foreseeable future. Recognizing these limits is crucial—not as a deterrent to innovation but as a guide to its responsible implementation.

As we transition into an era increasingly influenced by AI, the necessity for informed engagement becomes paramount. Education systems must transform to weave AI literacy into their foundations, preparing future generations to navigate and shape the AI-driven world. Policymaking, too, plays a central role, crafting frameworks that foster innovation while protecting individual rights and societal values.

This book seeks to bridge the gap between ignorance and understanding, offering an expository yet motivational narrative that empowers readers. By the conclusion, you'll approach AI not as a monolithic entity but as an intricate ecosystem ripe with possibility and caution. Our aim is not just to inform but to inspire active participation in the AI-disrupted landscape. Understanding the nuances of AI is no longer optional; it's a requisite for those determined to thrive in the 21st century. Through openness and inquiry, we illuminate a path forward where technology and humanity coexist harmoniously, charting a future that's both innovative and conscientious.

Chapter 1:
Understanding Artificial Intelligence

rtificial Intelligence, often shortened to AI, has swiftly transitioned from a concept nestled within the pages of science fiction to a tangible force that permeates every facet of contemporary life. It's not just a technological marvel but a transformative paradigm that's reshaping the way we see the world. AI systems are designed to mimic cognitive functions associated with the human mind, such as learning and problem-solving, enabling machines to perform tasks that once required human intelligence. Whether it's identifying patterns in vast sets of data or making autonomous decisions, AI has become a crucial catalyst for innovation. This chapter lays the foundation for our journey to understand AI's profound impact, demystifying the complexities while emphasizing its potential to shape our shared future. It's here where ideas are not just understood but also scrutinized, encouraging a dialogue about the balance between embracing new possibilities and addressing the societal challenges they present.

The History of AI

The journey into the world of artificial intelligence (AI) didn't start in the tech-driven landscapes of the 21st century. Its roots trace back to ancient myths and philosophical musings that envisioned intelligent automatons long before our modern ideas took shape. These early imaginations laid the groundwork for what would evolve into a pioneering field of study.

In the mid-20th century, AI began drawing serious attention from scholars and scientists. The era post-World War II, buzzing with scientific innovation and exploration, marked the dawn of a new understanding of machine capability. Alan Turing, a pivotal figure, introduced the notion of machines that could simulate any human intelligence task. His work on the Turing Test began challenging perceptions of machine and human boundaries, leading to fundamental inquiries into what intelligence truly means.

Despite the great enthusiasm, early AI faced hurdles, primarily due to limitations in computing power and data availability. Initial computers were slow, expensive, and lacked the storage necessary for complex problem-solving. In the 1950s and 1960s, AI research was largely theoretical, creating a foundation with mathematical algorithms and ideas but with little practical application.

Yet, it was in this period that AI established its name. The 1956 Dartmouth Conference, often credited as the birth of AI as a field, brought together key thinkers like John McCarthy, Marvin Minsky, Nathaniel Rochester, and Claude Shannon. Here, AI was officially named, and the concept of a machine capable of mimicking human intelligence was posited to the world.

The following decades, known as the "AI winters," were marked by periods of inflated expectations followed by harsh funding cuts and disillusionment. Researchers had promised advancements that technology could not yet support, leading to skepticism and dwindling financial backing. However, these setbacks were not in vain; instead, they spurred innovation, forcing scientists to re-evaluate and strengthen their approaches.

In the 1980s, AI witnessed a resurgence through the development of "expert systems." These were programs designed to mimic the decision-making ability of a human expert. Industries started harnessing AI for specific tasks, from diagnosing diseases to guiding oil-drilling processes. The commercial potential of AI became apparent, encouraging increased investment and interest.

Moving into the late 20th century, AI began to transform faster, driven by improvements in technology. With the advent of personal computers, computational power became more accessible, widening AI's practical reach. The emergence of the internet in the 1990s provided a wealth of data, fueling advancements and allowing AI to venture into new domains.

The explosion of data in the 21st century catalyzed an AI renaissance. Machine learning, a subset of AI, became a focal point for innovation. Algorithms capable of learning from vast datasets, such as neural networks, entered the mainstream, bringing about staggering advances. For instance, IBM's Watson defeated human champions on the quiz show "Jeopardy!" exemplifying AI's leap into functional intelligence.

One of the pivotal moments in AI's evolution was the 2016 victory of Google's AlphaGo over a world champion Go player. Go, an ancient and complex strategy game, had long been considered a formidable challenge for AI due to its vast possibilities and reliance on intuition over calculation. The victory showcased AI's potential in mastering sophisticated tasks, hinting at broader applications in real-world problem-solving.

Fast forward to today, AI is integrated into daily life in ways early pioneers could only dream of. From personal assistants like Siri and Alexa to autonomous vehicles, AI applications continue to grow in sophistication and ubiquity. This expansion has not only been technological but also philosophical. The once-niche discussions about

AI's implications are now central to debates about ethics, job market transformations, and societal shifts.

Furthermore, AI's journey is characterized by its collaborative nature. Global efforts have driven its progress, with governments, private sectors, and academia contributing to its evolving tapestry. This collaboration has accelerated AI's integration across fields, proving that while challenges remain, the potential benefits are manifold.

As we look ahead, understanding AI's history is crucial in navigating its future. It offers lessons in humility, reminding us of technology's unpredictable path and the necessity for continual adaptation and learning. AI's past, rich with trials and triumphs, lays a foundation from which society can introspectively and responsibly build onward.

The history of AI doesn't merely tell a story of technological evolution; it's a narrative about human ambition, curiosity, and resilience. It's a historical journey marked by dreams of possibility, moments of despair, and breakthroughs that redefined what machines and humans could achieve together. This legacy shapes our present understanding and our future endeavors, leading us into an age where AI holds the key to new realms of possibility.

Defining Artificial Intelligence

As we dive deeper into the realm of artificial intelligence (AI), it's essential to grasp a clear understanding of what AI truly entails. At its core, artificial intelligence is the development of computer systems that exhibit cognitive abilities traditionally associated with the human mind. These abilities include learning, reasoning, problem-solving, perception, and language understanding. These systems are designed to perform tasks that require human intelligence, and in some instances, they venture beyond what we as humans are naturally capable of achieving.

One fundamental aspect of AI is its ability to learn from data. Unlike traditional programs that follow predefined instructions, AI systems improve over time by analyzing patterns and outcomes. This adaptive learning process allows them to refine their operations, making them more effective as they process additional information. For instance, a language processing AI might start by recognizing simple patterns in sentence structure but eventually learn to understand complex linguistic nuances.

AI can be classified into different types based on its capabilities. Narrow AI, which we interact with frequently, excels at performing specific tasks like voice recognition or driving a car. This specialization makes it highly efficient but limits its application to the task it was designed for. For example, the AI in a personal assistant like Siri or Alexa is exceptional at understanding spoken commands, yet it doesn't possess the broad intelligence to write novels or compose symphonies.

On a more advanced level lies General AI, a theoretical construct that would mimic human intelligence in all aspects. Such an AI would theoretically be capable of any cognitive task a human can do—and possibly much more. However, this remains within the realm of theoretical exploration and speculation, as current research hasn't yet achieved this level of generalized understanding and adaptability.

Delving into the mechanics, AI utilizes several methodologies to emulate intelligent behavior. Machine learning, a subset of AI, provides systems with the ability to automatically learn and improve from experience without being explicitly programmed. Machine learning itself branches into supervised learning—where the system learns from a labeled dataset—and unsupervised learning, where it identifies patterns within unlabeled data.

A further layer of AI is deep learning, inspired by the neural architecture of the human brain. This approach uses neural networks to process data in complex ways, simulating a multi-layered understanding of information. Through deep learning, AI systems have achieved breakthroughs in image and speech recognition, surpassing the capabilities of traditional programming techniques.

In addition to machine and deep learning, AI encompasses areas like natural language processing, which enables machines to understand and respond to text or voice in a human-like manner. These systems have transformed our interaction with technology, making communication with machines more seamless and intuitive.

Artificial intelligence isn't a recent endeavor. The concept dates back to ancient times, with myths and stories featuring intelligent automata. However, the term "artificial intelligence" itself was coined in 1956 during a conference at Dartmouth College, marking the beginning of AI as a field of study. Since then, AI has evolved through peaks of optimism and valleys of skepticism—a phenomenon often referred to as "AI winters" and "AI springs."

Ethics also play a critical role in defining AI, as we ponder the responsibilities and implications of creating machines with potential autonomy. The development of AI raises fundamental questions about free will, consciousness, and the essence of being human. As AI systems become more sophisticated, the need for regulatory frameworks and ethical guidelines becomes imperative to ensure the beneficial evolution of AI technologies.

AI's influence permeates every aspect of modern life, from healthcare to finance to entertainment. Its definition continuously evolves as the technology advances and integrates deeper into our society. Therefore, understanding AI isn't just about knowing what it is today, but also anticipating what it can become tomorrow. The dynamic nature of AI ensures that its definition must remain fluid, adapting to innovations and societal changes.

As we explore the broader landscape of artificial intelligence, acknowledging its nuances allows us to appreciate both its potential and its limitations. Defining AI is not simply about identifying what it is capable of, but also about recognizing the profound impact it has on the way we live, work, and think.

Chapter 2:
The Evolution of Algorithms

Algorithms have journeyed from simple arithmetic rules to complex, adaptive systems that influence countless aspects of modern life. Early algorithms were painstakingly handcrafted, designed to perform specific tasks like basic calculations or sorting data. However, with the advent of digital computers, their potential expanded dramatically. This evolution accelerated as algorithms began incorporating principles of machine learning, enabling them to adapt and optimize without explicit programming. Unlike traditional software, where outputs are predictable based on predefined rules, today's algorithms often operate in a black-box fashion, analyzing massive datasets to 'learn' patterns and make decisions. As they become more integrated into the fabric of daily living—from tailoring our online experiences to driving autonomous vehicles—understanding their evolution empowers us to navigate their pervasive influence critically and thoughtfully.

Key Milestones in Algorithm Development

The journey through the evolution of algorithms is quite an intriguing one, marked by key milestones that have profoundly shaped how we interact with technology today. Let's embark on this exploration by tracing the roots back to their academic foundations and then watching as they unfurled into the pervasive forces they are now. This journey not only highlights the genius moments of human ingenuity but also reveals how algorithms became the backbone of a digital society.

Historically, algorithms date back centuries, with one of the earliest milestones being the development of the Euclidean Algorithm around 300 BC. This method for calculating the greatest common divisor of two numbers has stood the test of time, signifying how foundational concepts can influence diverse fields, from number theory to digital encryption. Fast forward to the 9th century, Al-Khwarizmi's work in "The Compendious Book on Calculation by Completion and Balancing" provided a systematic approach that eventually spawned the word "algorithm" itself. His contributions laid the groundwork for algebra, underscoring the pivotal role algorithms play in mathematical theory and practice.

The 20th century brought with it the advent of computational machines, heralding an era where algorithms transcended theoretical study and ventured into practical application. In 1936, Alan Turing's introduction of the Turing Machine conceptualized the notion of computation, establishing a framework for what would become computer science. His work paved the path for future developments, hinting at the potential of machines that could be systematically directed through algorithms to solve immensely complex problems.

Another watershed moment came in 1946 with the development of the ENIAC (Electronic Numerical Integrator and Computer), the first general-purpose electronic computer. This machine demonstrated that algorithms could harness computational power to perform extensive numerical calculations, a seminal step towards the automation we witness today. Algorithms were no longer static academic theories; they began to drive the machinery of innovation and efficiency.

As we navigated to the mid-20th century, the rise of artificial intelligence (AI) brought with it the promise of machines not just executing instructions but learning and adapting. A pivotal algorithmic leap occurred in 1956 with the formal declaration of artificial intelligence as a field during the Dartmouth Conference. Here, algorithms began evolving beyond rote calculation to become the architects of machine intelligence—a fundamental shift that redefined future technological ambitions.

Moving into the 1970s, the inception of the Fast Fourier Transform (FFT) algorithm marked another significant milestone. The work of Cooley and Tukey in developing a method for rapidly computing Fourier transforms revolutionized digital signal processing. Their contribution is now the cornerstone of data compression technologies, streaming multimedia, and various other innovations that hinge on efficiently processing large datasets.

During the 1990s, algorithms designed for web search engines entered the scene, exemplifying adaptation to the burgeoning digital information age. The PageRank algorithm, developed by Sergey Brin and Larry Page in 1996, utilized link relationships to determine the importance of web pages. This innovation was instrumental in launching Google and irrevocably altered how individuals could access information, cementing the integral role of algorithms in managing a knowledge-rich world.

The early 21st century witnessed a profound surge in machine learning algorithms, particularly with the advent of neural networks capable of deep learning. These algorithms mimic human brain function to recognize patterns, process natural language, and make decisions. The triumph of these algorithms was perhaps most memorably demonstrated in 2016 when Google DeepMind's AlphaGo defeated a world champion at Go—a complex game with more possible moves than there are atoms in the universe. This victory wasn't just about technical prowess; it symbolized the leap of algorithms into realms of strategic and intuitive capabilities, challenging the boundaries of human and machine potential.

We continue to witness the acceleration of algorithmic development, driven by the exponential growth of computation power and data availability. With quantum algorithms on the horizon, promising unprecedented processing capabilities, the story of algorithms is far from over. These milestones are not endpoints but stepping stones, supporting an ongoing evolution with impacts we're continuously exploring.

In reflection, these key milestones illustrate a rich tapestry of evolution—from early number theory to frontier-breaking AI applications—where algorithms transitioned from theoretical constructs to dynamic engines of change. As we live through a transformative era with algorithms embedded in nearly every facet of life, understanding their development reminds us of the profound ingenuity and curiosity that propel technological progress. It's a history that not only charts past achievements but also serves as a narrative guiding our future with digital and algorithmic intelligence.

Algorithms vs. Traditional Software

In the ever-evolving landscape of technology, algorithms have begun to outpace traditional software, ushering in a new era of computation. While both are central to how computers process and execute tasks, their underlying mechanisms and impacts differ profoundly. Traditional software, often built on rigid, rule-based logic, requires explicit instructions for every operation it performs. In contrast, algorithms, particularly those driving artificial intelligence, thrive on adaptability and learning, all while reshaping our interaction with technology.

Traditional software operates within the confines of determinism; it's akin to following a recipe where each step must be precisely defined. This type of software demands thorough upfront design and analysis, and its function rarely extends beyond its initial programming. Consider a word processor or a spreadsheet application—their scope is substantial, yet fundamentally limited by the confines of their coded instructions. This predictability forms the cornerstone of traditional software's reliability, yet it also imposes boundaries on flexibility and situational adaptability.

Conversely, algorithms allow for a form of evolution within software. They are not static; instead, they're dynamic pathways capable of adapting based on data inputs. Machine learning models, a subset of algorithms, can "learn" from historical data and identify patterns not explicitly programmed into them. This learning capacity propels algorithms beyond static instruction sets, enabling them to tackle complex problems with an almost human-like intuition. Such capability is transformative across multiple sectors, from personalized recommendations on streaming platforms to predictive analytics in finance.

In examining the divergence between algorithms and traditional software, one must consider not only the technological distinctions but also the philosophical and practical implications. Traditional software development is a testament to human ingenuity in logic and planning, where every potential condition must be accounted for. It upholds predictability and consistency as its highest virtues. Algorithms, however, introduce an element of autonomy through their capacity to independently derive solutions. They function more as collaborative entities rather than mere tools, requiring a new relationship between humans and technology.

The adaptive nature of algorithms extends their applicability in ways unimaginable in the era of traditional software. For example, autonomous vehicles rely heavily on complex algorithms to process real-time data and make split-second decisions that ensure safety and efficiency—a feat traditional software could hardly achieve due to its static nature. Moreover, the healthcare industry benefits from algorithm-driven diagnostics tools that can analyze vast amounts of medical data quickly and accurately, aiding in early disease detection and personalized treatment plans.

However, with great power comes great responsibility. The rise of algorithms necessitates a critical examination of bias, ethics, and accountability, as these algorithms often reflect the data they are trained on. While traditional software can have bugs corrected through precise code updates, algorithms require retraining and reevaluation, often demanding transparency in their decision-making processes. This necessity pushes developers and stakeholders to consider not only performance metrics but also ethical dimensions, such as fairness, transparency, and accountability.

Algorithms also challenge the traditional software development life cycle. Where once software updates were infrequent, driven by scheduled releases and patches, algorithm-driven systems often require continuous iteration and deployment. This paradigm shift emphasizes the importance of environments that allow for rapid experimentation and feedback loops, fostering a culture of perpetual improvement and innovation.

The comparison of traditional software and algorithms is not merely an academic exercise. It has profound implications for how we design, use, and regulate technology. As society increasingly depends on algorithm-driven decision-making, it becomes crucial to understand the limitations and opportunities that such systems present. Traditional software won't disappear; it will continue to serve foundational roles that value stability and straightforwardness. But algorithms, with their vast potential to learn and evolve, promise to drive the next wave of technological advancement.

Ultimately, the coexistence of algorithms and traditional software embodies the duality of the digital age. Each has its merits and limitations, shaping different aspects of our human-tech interaction. The future likely holds a synergy where traditional software frameworks provide a stable infrastructure, while algorithms add the flexibility and adaptability necessary for progress in a world defined by change.

Chapter 3:
AI in Daily Life

As we progress into a world increasingly woven with technology, artificial intelligence (AI) permeates our daily routines in ways both subtle and profound. From the moment we wake to smart alarms that adapt to our sleep patterns, to the predictive algorithms that curate our morning news, AI has become an unassuming personal assistant. It learns our preferences and habits, powering the devices and applications that make life more convenient. With AI, our homes transform into intelligent environments where thermostats adjust themselves and lights respond to our presence, enhancing comfort and energy efficiency. These invisible, yet indispensable, AI systems gracefully blend into the background, quietly orchestrating the symphony of our lives, as we go about our day, often unaware of the complex computations happening at our fingertips. This seamless integration is only the beginning of AI's journey in redefining what normal life looks like, inviting us to reflect on its growing role and the responsibilities it entails.

AI in Home Automation

As we continue our journey into the realms of artificial intelligence in our daily lives, home automation emerges as one of the most transformative applications of AI technologies. This intersection of machine learning, connectivity, and smart devices has reshaped how we interact with our living spaces. Imagine walking into a home that intuitively knows your preferences, adjusting settings seamlessly to enhance your comfort, security, and energy efficiency.

The concept of home automation isn't entirely new. It's been evolving over the past few decades. Early examples included basic programmable thermostats and simple remote controls. However, it's the integration of AI that has propelled home automation systems to a level of sophistication previously reserved for science fiction. Today, smart homes do more than just respond to commands—they anticipate needs, learn habits, and make adjustments autonomously.

One of the key drivers behind AI-powered home automation is the ability of devices to learn from data. Machine learning algorithms can analyze patterns from homeowner interactions, identifying when to adjust the lighting, heating, or even play your favorite music as you walk through the door. This learning capability is where AI distinguishes itself, turning passive devices into active participants in day-to-day routines.

Consider the smart thermostat as a classic example of AI in home automation. A device like the Nest Learning Thermostat goes beyond scheduling your heating and cooling. It observes how you adjust your thermostat over time. By analyzing this data, the system identifies patterns and begins to automatically make energy-saving decisions. This not only keeps your home comfortable but also reduces energy consumption significantly, contributing to environmental sustainability.

Furthermore, AI in home automation provides unprecedented control and flexibility through virtual assistants such as Amazon's Alexa, Google Assistant, and Apple's Siri. These voice-activated AI systems integrate with numerous smart home devices, allowing users to control their environment with simple voice commands. By making these systems intuitive and accessible, AI helps break down the barriers of technology interaction, empowering all members of a household.

Security remains a pivotal concern when discussing AI in smart homes. AI-enhanced security systems are becoming the standard, as they can offer real-time monitoring and quick responses to potential threats. Take smart cameras, for instance, equipped with AI for facial recognition and anomaly detection. They can differentiate between family members and strangers, reducing the number of false alerts and enhancing overall home security.

Interestingly, the integration of AI doesn't just mean more advanced tech—it means a more personalized living experience. AI-driven home automation learns about personal tastes and habits, from the perfect time to adjust the blinds to the ideal volume for evening relaxation. These systems can even remind you to take an umbrella if it anticipates rain—a small gesture, but one that epitomizes the potential of AI to blend seamlessly into our lives.

Of course, the array of smart devices involved in home automation raises concerns about privacy and data security. Every connected device is a potential entry point for cyber threats. Therefore, ensuring the security of AI systems in home automation is as crucial as the comfort and convenience they bring. Companies developing these technologies must prioritize data encryption and robust security protocols to protect users.

The development of AI in home automation stands as a testament to the power of collaborative innovation. Technological advancements in sensors, machine learning, and connectivity come together to create environments that are responsive and adaptive. As more people embrace smart home technology, it's apparent that the quest is not just about intelligent controls but about seamless integration into our daily lives.

Looking ahead, the role of AI in home automation will likely extend beyond individual homes to communities and cities. Imagine residential areas where energy usage is optimized across homes, or where local weather conditions predictively influence energy management. As AI systems become more interconnected, the potential for creating smarter, more sustainable living environments grows exponentially.

In essence, AI in home automation is redefining our notion of living spaces. It's about creating a symbiotic relationship between us and our homes—one where technology doesn't feel like an intruder but a welcomed participant. As we continue to push the boundaries of what's possible, AI has the potential to transform not only how we live but how we perceive the very essence of home.

Personal Assistants and AI

In the age of smart technology, personal assistants powered by artificial intelligence have redefined convenience. These digital aides, such as Amazon's Alexa, Google Assistant, and Apple's Siri, have become more than just helpful household devices — they're pivotal components in managing our daily lives. And yet, how have they become so integral, and what does this mean for our future? These personal assistants are a testament to AI's remarkable capability to understand and process human language, respond to queries, and even predict needs, showcasing the seamless interaction between humans and machines.

From setting alarms and reminders to managing smart home appliances, these AI-driven bots take on tasks that might otherwise consume our time and attention. They're designed to learn from our behaviors and preferences, adapting to each user's unique style and needs. This level of personalization not only enhances efficiency but also builds a sense of familiarity between the user and their digital assistant. It's like having a personal concierge who knows your schedule, anticipates your routine, and removes barriers between intention and action.

Yet, the journey of AI assisting in our personal lives is not without its challenges and implications. One significant consideration is the privacy and security of personal data. Personal assistants require access to vast amounts of personal information to function effectively, raising questions about where this data goes and how it is protected. Are these devices listening all the time? What kind of data are they collecting? These questions encourage a deeper look into how we can safeguard our privacy while enjoying the benefits AI offers.

Additionally, the efficiency and allure of personal assistants come from their ability to process natural language — an incredibly complex task for machines. This requires sophisticated algorithms capable of parsing not just words but context, tone, and intent. Personal assistants have made immense advancements in natural language processing, allowing them to handle varied accents, dialects, and languages more efficiently than ever before. However, they are not infallible, often requiring user corrections and input to improve accuracy over time.

Moreover, the integration of AI personal assistants into daily routines exemplifies how AI has infiltrated not only our homes but the broader fabric of society. Their increasing role in day-to-day activities also brings to light discussions about dependency and the potential loss of skills, as we hand over more of our tasks to machines. With every shopping list dictated and every calendar event scheduled by AI, there's a growing concern about the impact on our cognitive abilities and decision-making skills.

Despite these concerns, there is significant potential for personal assistants to evolve and further enrich our lives. Consider the role of AI in elder care, assisting those with disabilities, or even facilitating education by providing access to information with ease. These devices can offer companionship and aid, particularly to those who might otherwise feel isolated or overwhelmed by technological advancements.

With every technological leap, the landscape of AI in our private spheres grows more dynamic. Developers and researchers continually strive to enhance the capabilities, accuracy, and intuitiveness of these personal assistants, aiming to make them indispensable companions in both mundane and complex tasks. It's a field that's growing rapidly, driven by a wave of innovations and discoveries in AI technology.

Looking forward, we face the challenge of balancing the undeniable convenience of personal assistants with ethical considerations and societal impacts. Ensuring that the data powering these improvements are used responsibly and transparently is crucial. As users become more reliant on such technologies, striking a balance between utility and privacy will define the next phase of AI personal assistants in our lives.

Ultimately, the evolution of personal assistants in AI is a mirror reflecting our relationship with technology. It demonstrates our desire for tools that simplify and enhance our daily routines while highlighting the ongoing dialog about privacy, ethical use, and the transformative power of artificial intelligence. As these assistants become more capable, empathetic, and integrated, they may not only change the way we live but also influence the manner in which we interact with the world around us.

Chapter 4:
Algorithms at Work

In modern workplaces, algorithms constantly operate behind the scenes, influencing decisions and shaping workflows in ways we often overlook. From optimizing supply chains to personalizing marketing strategies, they're becoming indispensable tools for efficiency and innovation. These digital maestros process vast amounts of data at lightning speed, detecting patterns that would elude any human eye. In doing so, they're transforming roles and responsibilities, redefining productivity, and sometimes sparking debates about job displacement and workplace fairness. As we adapt to this algorithm-driven environment, the key lies in understanding how these invisible forces function and finding a balance where human creativity and algorithmic logic can thrive together. By grasping their potential and pitfalls, we can better navigate the evolving landscape where man and machine collaborate to drive progress.

AI in the Workplace

Artificial Intelligence (AI) has undeniably reshaped the modern workplace, infiltrating industries with unparalleled speed and efficiency. This shift isn't a mere incremental technological upgrade; it represents a fundamental transformation in how businesses operate, make decisions, and interact with their employees and customers. AI has become a strategic partner in today's organizational landscape, enabling companies to boost productivity, streamline operations, and make data-driven decisions with more accuracy and less human intervention than ever before.

The workplace dynamic is evolving as AI takes on tasks that were once squarely within the human domain. Routine and mundane activities, from scheduling to data entry, are increasingly automated, freeing employees to focus on more creative and complex challenges. In customer service, AI-driven chatbots and virtual assistants are not only improving response times but also enhancing customer interactions by providing personalized solutions. This evolution demonstrates AI's capacity to augment human abilities, allowing employees to work smarter and more efficiently.

Yet, the introduction of AI into the workplace also brings its own set of challenges. There's the perennial concern of job displacement. People worry about automation rendering certain roles obsolete, particularly those involving repetitive tasks. However, while some jobs are certainly at risk, AI has also created a multitude of new roles requiring human skills that machines can't replicate—like empathy, leadership, and strategic thinking. It's becoming increasingly evident that the future workplace will rely heavily on synergies between human intellect and AI capabilities.

Moreover, AI has forced a reevaluation of skills considered essential in the job market. As AI takes on more decision-making tasks, critical thinking, problem-solving, and emotional intelligence rise in value. Professional development now often includes upskilling programs focused on these areas, alongside technical competencies required for operating and interacting with AI systems. Companies investing in workforce development initiatives not only enhance their adaptability but also reinforce their commitment to a sustainable AI-human collaboration in the workplace.

Incorporating AI into the workplace doesn't stop at efficiency; it also transforms corporate strategy and culture. Decisions that were once made based solely on human intuition or past experiences now have the backup of real-time data analytics, pattern recognition, and predictive modeling. This shift towards evidence-based decision-making alters organizational dynamics, encouraging a culture of transparency and continual improvement. AI's capacity to process vast amounts of data and deliver actionable insights shifts how leaders evaluate risk, measure success, and drive innovation.

Different industries have shown varying levels of adaptation to AI tools. In manufacturing, AI optimizes supply chains and enhances predictive maintenance, thereby reducing downtime and operational costs. Finance sectors use AI for fraud detection and credit scoring, facilitating more secure transactions and fairer lending practices. Meanwhile, in sectors like marketing and sales, AI-driven insights into consumer behavior allow for more targeted and effective campaigns, enhancing customer engagement.

However, with AI's integration into the workplace also comes the need for robust ethical frameworks to address concerns surrounding privacy, bias, and transparency. The algorithms driving AI systems must be designed and implemented with a conscious understanding of their potential impacts on employees and customers alike. Companies adopting AI must ensure that their technological solutions uphold principles of fairness and do not exacerbate existing inequalities or inadvertently create new ones.

As AI continues to mature, the lines between human roles and machine capabilities will blur further. This evolution doesn't just stimulate productivity; it inspires innovative solutions to complex challenges and enables personalized experiences at scale. The companies that will thrive in this new era are those that embrace change, foster a learning-centric environment, and view AI as a tool to amplify human potential rather than replace it.

The workplace of tomorrow will likely look vastly different from today, yet at its core will remain a commitment to collaboration and the shared goal of advancing human possibilities through technology. In embracing this change, organizations not only stay competitive in a rapidly changing environment but also contribute to building a world in which human creativity and AI-driven efficiency come together in harmony.

Thus, the future isn't about AI taking over the human role but about a collaborative partnership where each contributes its strengths to achieve what neither could alone. This partnership will define the progressive workplaces of the future, characterized by resilience, adaptability, and a shared vision of sustainable growth.

In summary, AI's role in the workplace marks a significant juncture in the evolution of work itself. As it continues to permeate various industries, organizations must navigate both its opportunities and challenges. By fostering environments that empower employees to grow alongside technological advances, businesses can truly harness the transformative power of AI, not just for efficiency, but as a catalyst for innovation and growth.

The Gig Economy and Algorithms

The gig economy has emerged as a transformative force in the modern workforce, redefining traditional employment frameworks and shifting the nature of work itself. This shift is largely facilitated by algorithms, which have become the invisible drivers behind platforms that offer gig work opportunities. The marriage of the gig economy and algorithms is reshaping labor markets, affecting everything from how work is assigned to how workers are evaluated. But what does this really mean for workers, employers, and the underlying economic structure?

At its core, the gig economy is characterized by short-term, flexible jobs often mediated by digital platforms. Unlike traditional jobs that typically come with benefits and security, gig work is more fluid, providing both opportunities and challenges. Algorithms play a pivotal role in this space, primarily by matching supply and demand. For instance, ride-hailing services like Uber and Lyft use sophisticated algorithms to pair drivers with riders, determining routes, pricing, and even how drivers are rated.

These algorithms do more than just facilitate transactions; they have profound implications for power dynamics in the workforce. By controlling the flow of opportunities and revenue, algorithms hold significant sway over gig workers' livelihoods. For example, dynamic pricing algorithms adjust fare rates based on demand, but such adjustments often lack transparency, leaving drivers uncertain about their potential earnings at any given time.

The gig economy offers unique flexibility, allowing workers to choose when and where they work. For some, this means better work-life balance and the ability to pursue multiple opportunities simultaneously. However, this flexibility comes at a cost. Gig workers often face unpredictable incomes and limited access to traditional employment benefits like health insurance, retirement plans, and paid leave. The responsibility of managing these aspects falls on the individual rather than the employer.

Algorithms also introduce new forms of surveillance and control. Gig platforms meticulously track worker activity, collecting data on location, hours worked, customer interactions, and performance metrics. While this data can be used to improve service quality and efficiency, it can also lead to intrusive monitoring and stringent performance requirements. Consequently, the agency of workers in the gig economy can be compromised, as constant monitoring often influences behavior and decision-making.

Critics argue that the prevalence of algorithm-driven platforms in the gig economy exacerbates existing inequalities. Workers with higher ratings or longer tenures on these platforms may receive preferential treatment, while newcomers or those with lower ratings may struggle to find opportunities. Furthermore, algorithmic biases—whether inadvertent or systemic—can lead to discrimination, as algorithms may inadvertently penalize individuals based on geographic location, cultural backgrounds, or availability.

Despite the challenges, there is room for optimism regarding the potential improvements algorithms can bring to the gig economy. For one, advancements in algorithm transparency can empower workers, enabling them to understand how decisions are made and how they can influence outcomes. Moreover, fairer algorithmic designs could foster equitable opportunities, ensuring all workers have a level playing field.

There is also a growing recognition that policies and regulation must evolve to address the unique needs of gig workers. Policymakers around the world are beginning to explore how traditional labor laws might adapt to new employment landscapes, ensuring gig workers are afforded necessary protections without stifling the innovation that makes the gig economy attractive and dynamic.

For employers and platform operators, creating ethical and responsible algorithms isn't just about compliance or reputation; it's about sustainability. As public scrutiny of gig platforms increases, there's a mounting need to build systems that prioritize fairness, worker well-being, and corporate accountability.

As we look to the future, the relationship between the gig economy and algorithms will likely deepen, influenced by advances in artificial intelligence and machine learning. These technologies promise to make algorithms more predictive and adaptive, potentially enhancing the efficiency of gig work systems. However, with these advancements come the imperative to address the ethical implications and ensure that human interests remain at the forefront.

The gig economy, powered by algorithms, is reshaping our understanding of work in profound ways. By navigating its complexities and embracing both its challenges and opportunities, we stand to redefine what employment means in the 21st century. How we address these issues will ultimately determine the gig economy's impact on our society and the livelihoods of millions who find their vocation within its digital confines.

Chapter 5:
AI in Healthcare

A I is transforming healthcare, heralding a new era where complex diagnostics and patient care become more efficient and personalized. Imagine a world where early diagnosis of diseases, even before symptoms manifest, becomes the norm—AI makes this a reality through advanced imaging and pattern recognition systems. Healthcare providers now have algorithms as allies, interpreting vast datasets to assist in pinpointing potential health risks. This heralds not only improved patient outcomes but also a redefined patient experience, making healthcare more proactive than reactive. Yet, while AI's role promises remarkable advancements, it's vital to remain vigilant about ethical considerations, ensuring these technologies complement rather than replace the crucial human touch. The potential of AI in healthcare is boundless, urging us to craft a future where technology and humanity thrive together.

Advances in Medical Diagnostics

Artificial intelligence is reshaping countless industries, but perhaps none so profoundly as healthcare. At the heart of this transformation is the unassuming yet revolutionary field of medical diagnostics. AI's entry into this domain is both a technological leap and an ethical quandary, creating opportunities and challenges in equal measure. In this section, we explore how AI, with its blend of algorithms and data processing power, is advancing medical diagnostics and what it means for the future of healthcare.

Traditional methods of diagnosing diseases often rely on a complex interplay of visual inspections, subjective assessments, and manual tests. While effective to a certain degree, these methods are inherently limited by human variance and time constraints. Enter AI: a technology capable of analyzing massive datasets quickly and accurately, thereby enhancing diagnostic precision and reducing the chances of human error. AI algorithms can sift through medical images such as X-rays, MRIs, and CT scans, identifying patterns and abnormalities that might elude even the most trained human eye.

Consider the case of radiology, a field that has seen dramatic changes due to AI advancements. Radiologists are tasked with interpreting vast numbers of medical images daily, a feat that demands both time and keen attention. AI algorithms can assist by pre-screening these images, highlighting potential areas of concern, and thus allowing radiologists to focus on more nuanced analysis. This collaboration not only speeds up the diagnostic process but also adds an extra layer of confidence, where AI-driven analytics support human expertise.

Another area witnessing substantial AI-driven progress is pathology. Pathological diagnosis has traditionally involved scrutinizing tissue samples to detect disease. However, AI now offers enhanced diagnostic capabilities through computational pathology, which uses machine learning models to interpret microscopic images. These AI tools can provide pathologists with insights into cellular patterns and disease markers, facilitating early and accurate disease detection.

The realm of genomics also benefits significantly from AI's diagnostic prowess. As genomics involves the analysis of large-scale genomic data sets to determine genetic predispositions to diseases, AI's ability to process and interpret complex datasets is invaluable. AI algorithms can identify gene mutations associated with specific diseases, predict patient responses to treatment, and even suggest personalized therapeutic strategies. This capability paves the way for precision medicine, where treatments and care pathways are tailor-made for individuals based on their genetic makeup.

AI's impact isn't limited to imaging and genomics; it extends into other facets of medical diagnostics, such as predictive analytics. By analyzing electronic health records (EHRs), AI can predict patient outcomes and potential health risks. These predictive models look beyond the present, offering insights into future health scenarios. For instance, AI algorithms can evaluate historical patient data to foresee the likelihood of conditions like heart disease or diabetes, enabling proactive healthcare interventions.

Despite its promise, the integration of AI in medical diagnostics raises significant ethical and practical concerns. The reliance on AI demands robust data privacy and security measures, particularly when dealing with sensitive health information. Ensuring that patient data is protected while leveraging AI's full potential is a delicate balance. Furthermore, there's the challenge of algorithmic bias, where the AI's conclusions might reflect the biases present in its training data. This leads to questions about the fairness and impartiality of AI-enhanced diagnostic tools.

There's also the matter of how healthcare providers and patients perceive and trust AI diagnostics. While AI can process vast amounts of data more efficiently than a human, understanding and confidence in its decisions are crucial. Patients might be skeptical of an AI-provided diagnosis without a human's personal touch. Hence, there's a need for transparency in AI algorithms to build trust and ensure that they function as useful aids to healthcare professionals, not as replacements.

Nevertheless, the potential of AI to democratize healthcare by making diagnostics more accessible and affordable is immense. In regions with limited access to specialists or advanced medical technologies, AI can bridge the gap. Mobile health applications powered by AI can offer preliminary diagnoses, triaging patients and directing them to the appropriate care levels. This capability is particularly vital in developing countries and rural areas, where healthcare resources are often scarce.

Furthermore, the continuous evolution of AI technology promises even more sophisticated diagnostic capabilities in the future. New algorithms are being developed to enhance the accuracy of AI predictions, integrate multimodal data, and support real-time diagnostics. As research in AI-driven diagnostics progresses, we can anticipate even more groundbreaking discoveries that will redefine the healthcare landscape.

In conclusion, AI's advances in medical diagnostics symbolize a new era in healthcare—one with the potential to deliver faster, more accurate, and more accessible diagnostic services. However, the success of this revolution depends heavily on our ability to address the ethical, privacy, and trust issues that accompany it. As we embrace these technological innovations, the focus must remain on ensuring that AI serves as a tool for enhancing human health rather than supplanting human judgment. With careful implementation and ongoing vigilance, AI will undoubtedly be a powerful ally in the quest for improved healthcare outcomes.

AI in Patient Care

Artificial Intelligence (AI) in patient care marks a significant evolution in how healthcare is delivered. It's transforming the landscape of patient interaction, offering personalized care, enhancing treatment outcomes, and reshaping the dynamics between patients and healthcare providers. At the core of this transformation lies the ability of AI systems to process vast amounts of data swiftly and accurately. This prowess assists doctors and nurses, enabling them to spend more time on complex decision-making and direct patient care while leaving routine tasks to the machines.

Let's start by delving into one of the most promising aspects of AI in patient care—personalization. Healthcare isn't one-size-fits-all. Every patient has a unique genetic makeup, lifestyle, and health history. AI leverages data analytics to understand and predict individual patient needs. Sophisticated algorithms can analyze records, medical history, and even lifestyle choices to tailor treatment plans. This level of personalized medicine isn't just futuristic; it's happening now, allowing for treatments that are both effective and efficient.

AI-driven tools are reshaping diagnostic processes as well. Algorithms trained on thousands of medical images can identify patterns and anomalies that might be invisible to the human eye. For example, AI is already outperforming seasoned radiologists in detecting certain types of cancers at early stages. This doesn't mean replacing doctors but augmenting their abilities. By taking over the heavy lifting of sifting through data and imagery, AI allows clinicians to direct their expertise toward nuanced interpretation and patient interaction.

Precision medicine, powered by AI, is another crucial piece of the puzzle. This involves customizing healthcare, with medical decisions and treatments tailored to the individual patient rather than a generic approach. AI models analyze enormous datasets, encompassing genetic data, to predict how individual patients will respond to specific treatments. Such insights enable doctors to prescribe medications that are more likely to be effective, reducing the trial-and-error method's need and minimizing side effects.

Beyond diagnostics and treatment personalization, AI is redefining the patient engagement paradigm. Chatbots and virtual assistants are emerging as central figures in patient interaction. They provide 24/7 support, answer medical queries, remind patients about medication, and even assist with scheduling appointments. By automating these routine tasks, healthcare providers can focus more on delivering high-quality care. It's not just administrative efficiencies; these AI tools enhance patient experience, offering a sense of empowerment and involvement in their health journey.

AI's influence doesn't stop at the clinic or hospital. For patients with chronic conditions, AI-powered home monitoring systems are a game changer. They track vital signs, alerting both patients and caregivers to potential health concerns before they become critical. For instance, wearable technology equipped with AI can monitor heart rate, blood pressure, and glucose levels in real-time. Such proactive care management decreases hospital readmissions and improves quality of life for patients managing long-term illnesses.

While AI holds vast potential, it's crucial to address the ethical and practical concerns arising from its use in patient care. Data privacy stands as a foremost concern. AI systems require access to patient data to function effectively, which brings into question data handling, storage, and security. Transparency in how this data is used and whether it's anonymized is essential to maintain trust. Moreover, the interpretation of data by AI models must be clear and comprehensible, allowing healthcare providers and patients to understand the rationale behind medical recommendations.

The integration of AI in patient care also prompts questions about accountability. If an AI system misdiagnoses or suggests an ineffective treatment, who's responsible? Establishing lines of accountability is critical as AI becomes more embedded in decision-making processes. Collaboration between AI developers, healthcare providers, and policymakers will be essential to navigate these complex ethical landscapes and build frameworks that protect patient interests.

Training and adaptability are equally important considerations. Healthcare professionals must be equipped with the skills and knowledge to leverage AI technologies effectively. This includes understanding AI's capabilities, limitations, and how best to integrate them into patient care protocols. Education and ongoing professional development tailored to these emerging technologies are vital to ensure that AI enhances rather than hinders patient care.

Despite challenges, the potential benefits of AI in patient care are hard to ignore. By continuing to refine and safely integrate these technologies, healthcare systems can evolve to meet the complex needs of modern patient care. AI allows healthcare to transition from reactive to proactive, where early interventions prevent complications and health concerns are managed efficiently. Ultimately, it's about creating a holistic healthcare ecosystem where patients receive the best possible care, underpinned by technology that amplifies human insight and compassion.

AI in patient care isn't just a technological advance; it's a paradigm shift towards precision, efficiency, and patient-centered focus. By embracing these advancements with a vigilant eye on ethics and implementation, we can step into a new era of healthcare—one that delivers better outcomes through intelligent, data-driven decision-making.

Chapter 6:
AI and the Media

In a world where information is as pervasive as air, artificial intelligence transforms the media landscape in ways previously unimaginable. AI is not just a tool but a silent architect, reshaping how news is curated, disseminated, and consumed. Algorithms now decide which stories land on our screens, prioritizing engagement sometimes at the cost of truth. This power shift raises concerns about echo chambers, misinformation, and the erosion of unbiased reporting. Yet, AI also holds promise, offering innovative tools for investigative journalism and personalized content delivery. As society navigates this complex terrain, the challenge lies in fostering a media environment that upholds integrity while embracing the efficiency and reach that AI offers. Balancing these forces demands not only technological oversight but a renewed commitment to ethical journalism, where human values guide algorithmic decision-making. In doing so, we can harness AI's potential to enrich the narrative of our shared human experience.

The Role of Algorithms in News Distribution

In today's digital world, algorithms play a crucial role in how news is distributed and consumed. This development has transformed the traditional landscape of news, making it more dynamic, personalized, and instantaneous. As algorithms curate news feeds tailored to an individual's interests, they're constantly reshaping the flow of information. This process is not just technical but profoundly impacts society, affecting everything from personal knowledge to public discourse.

At the heart of algorithm-driven news distribution lies the idea of personalization. Algorithms analyze vast stores of data, drawing from past user behaviors, clicks, shares, and likes. Based on this data, they tailor the news content that each user sees. This customization aims to keep readers engaged by showing them stories they find interesting or relevant. However, this personalized experience is double-edged. While it can enhance user satisfaction by filtering out noise, it also raises concerns about the creation of "filter bubbles." In these bubbles, users encounter only viewpoints that reinforce their existing beliefs, potentially limiting exposure to diverse perspectives.

The sheer volume of information processed by these algorithms cannot be overstated. Every day, millions of articles, blog posts, and social media updates compete for attention. Algorithms sift through this ocean of content to highlight the most pertinent pieces for individual users. This task, executed at rapid speeds and vast scales, represents a profound shift from traditional editorial-based systems where a human editor selected front-page news. The power has effectively shifted from human editors to machine-driven decisions, altering the dynamics of newsrooms across the globe.

Machine learning plays a pivotal role in refining news distribution algorithms. Through continuous learning processes, algorithms become increasingly adept at predicting user preferences. These systems can improve over time, optimizing which articles, videos, or posts will appear in a user's feed. Yet, at the same time, the opaque nature of these algorithms remains a significant concern. Users rarely understand how or why specific pieces of news are prioritized. This lack of transparency fuels suspicion and skepticism over whether algorithms can be trusted to serve the public good.

Moreover, the role of algorithms in news distribution isn't just about selecting content but also about timing and presentation. For instance, algorithms determine not just which stories appear on a news feed but also when they appear and in what order. The subtle yet profound effects of such decisions can influence public opinion and behavior. They can, for instance, amplify the visibility of breaking news during peak hours or bury controversial stories during lulls, subtly shaping the public dialogue.

Yet, it's not just about how the news is filtered; it's also about who controls these algorithms. Typically, large tech companies own and operate them, wielding tremendous influence over public access to information. Critics argue that this concentrated power can lead to conflicts of interest where economic motives supersede the commitment to unbiased news dissemination. As a result, calls for regulation and more democratic control over news algorithms are gaining momentum.

Despite the challenges, there's no denying the potential benefits of algorithmic news distribution. When executed with care and responsibility, these systems can democratize information, making it more accessible to broader audiences. They have the power to support informed citizenry by tailoring complex data into more digestible formats while preserving accuracy and context. Furthermore, algorithms can highlight underreported stories, giving a voice to marginalized communities and bringing attention to critical issues often overshadowed in traditional media.

The evolution of news algorithms is also transforming journalism itself. Journalists now find themselves working alongside data scientists to understand how stories travel online. There is a growing emphasis on "data journalism," where analytical tools help to create meaningful narratives around raw data. This collaboration can enhance reports' depth and accuracy but also shifts journalists' focus towards optimizing content for algorithmic recommendations. Balancing journalistic integrity with the demands of the digital age remains an ongoing challenge.

As we navigate this landscape, an important question emerges: how can society ensure that these algorithms serve the public interest? Subsidiary to this are issues surrounding bias, propaganda, and the manipulation of news algorithms for political or economic gain. Building algorithms that incorporate ethical considerations and prioritize truthfulness over sensationalism is paramount. Initiatives like algorithmic audits and the establishment of standardized ethical frameworks aspire to create systems accountable to public scrutiny.

Moreover, fostering digital literacy among users plays a critical role. Educating individuals about how algorithms influence the news they consume empowers them to seek out diverse sources actively. Encouraging users to question and critically engage with content is essential to counteract the echo chambers that these systems may inadvertently create. Recognizing the signs of manipulative or skewed representation and opting for a rich tapestry of viewpoints strengthens democratic participation.

The future of algorithmic news distribution portends advancements that could further revolutionize how we consume information. Artificial intelligence is rapidly evolving towards more sophisticated natural language processing capabilities, potentially offering more nuanced and insightful content curation. As AI systems become better at understanding context, sentiment, and subtext, the algorithms of tomorrow might offer even more relevant and engaging news experiences while challenging us to uphold democratic values in their design and application.

Ultimately, the role of algorithms in news distribution is a testament to the challenges and opportunities at the intersection of technology and society. While they hold incredible potential to revolutionize news access, the road ahead demands careful navigation. It requires collaboration between technologists, policymakers, media organizations, and the public to ensure that the flow of information remains a force for good, empowering individuals with knowledge and truth in an increasingly connected world.

Social Media and AI

The interplay between social media and artificial intelligence has transformed the digital landscape. Social media platforms have become ubiquitous, a constant companion in our daily lives. They have reshaped the way we communicate, consume news, and even how we perceive the world. At the heart of this metamorphosis lies AI, a quiet yet powerful presence that influences what we see, share, and engage with online.

AI-driven algorithms curate our feeds with remarkable precision. They sift through mountains of data to predict what content will keep us scrolling, commenting, and liking. By analyzing patterns in user behavior, these algorithms tailor experiences unique to each user. This personalization stems from more than just a series of calculations; it involves a deep understanding of user engagement metrics, preferences, and trends derived from massive datasets. The result is a digital ecosystem finely tuned to capture attention, often without us even realizing it.

However, the seamless integration of AI into social media comes with its set of challenges. One of the most significant issues is the creation of echo chambers, where users are continually exposed to content that aligns with their pre-existing beliefs. These spaces often amplify biases and foster polarization, as algorithms prioritize content that triggers engagement—even if it's at the expense of balanced perspectives. The repercussions of such algorithmic choices extend beyond online interactions, influencing societal ideologies and fueling divisions.

Despite these challenges, AI also offers unprecedented opportunities for innovation within social media. For instance, it can enhance user experience through intuitive interfaces and adaptive content. Advanced natural language processing techniques enable AI to understand and respond to user queries more accurately than ever before. Chatbots powered by AI engage with users in real-time, handling customer service requests and providing personalized recommendations that enhance user satisfaction.

Moreover, AI plays a crucial role in content moderation. Given the sheer volume of posts generated every day, manual moderation is a daunting task. AI algorithms, trained on diverse datasets, can identify and flag inappropriate or harmful content efficiently and at scale. This automated vigilance is crucial in maintaining safe digital spaces, especially in times when misinformation can spread rapidly and have real-world implications.

However, relying too heavily on AI for moderation comes with its limitations. Algorithms can misinterpret nuanced contexts, sometimes flagging innocuous content as harmful or letting damaging material slip through. The key is finding a balance between human oversight and AI efficiency, ensuring that platforms remain spaces conducive to safe and constructive dialogue.

The aesthetic side of social media too has been revolutionized by AI. Filters that beautify images, generate unique artistic styles, or animate our expressions have become possible due to sophisticated machine learning models. These tools, once considered advanced technology, are now standard features in social applications, allowing users to creatively express themselves in novel ways.

AI also underpins the influencer ecosystem that thrives on social media. By analyzing engagement data, marketers and influencers can optimize their strategies to maximize reach and impact. AI tools evaluate metrics such as follower demographics, engagement rates, and sentiment analysis to streamline marketing efforts. This enables brands to connect with targeted audiences more effectively, transforming social media into powerful marketing platforms.

Yet, as AI continues to weave itself into the fabric of social media, it raises critical questions about privacy, agency, and control. Users often unknowingly share swathes of personal data that feeds AI algorithms. This data is then utilized for targeted advertising, raising concerns about privacy invasion. Moreover, the opacity of many algorithms means users rarely understand how their online personas are shaped and manipulated, sparking debates over autonomy in the digital sphere.

Certainly, AI's integration with social media is not without ethical considerations. As platforms scramble to monetize their services through data-driven advertising, the need for transparent policies becomes paramount. It is essential for users to have a clear understanding of how their data is used, with fail-safes in place to prevent misuse. This necessitates not only technological solutions but robust policy frameworks governing the ethical use of AI in social media.

Another promising area where AI is making strides is in broadening accessibility. AI-powered captioning, translation services, and voice-assisted navigation make social media more inclusive, enabling users with disabilities to engage more fully with content across global boundaries. These tools not only democratize access to information but also enrich interactions among diverse users, fostering an inclusive digital environment.

As we continue to navigate the evolving terrain of social media, the relationship between these platforms and AI will only deepen. The challenges we face are significant, but so are the opportunities for innovation and improvement. It's crucial to actively engage with these technologies, questioning not just how they shape our experiences but also leveraging them to create a more equitable digital future. In doing so, we can ensure that the convergence of social media and AI reflects our highest aspirations for connectedness, understanding, and community.

Chapter 7:
AI in Education

The landscape of education is undergoing a transformative shift with the integration of artificial intelligence, bringing new opportunities and challenges into the classroom. AI empowers personalized learning experiences through adaptive learning technologies, which tailor instructional content to meet the unique needs and pace of each student. This customization promises to bridge gaps in understanding and facilitate a deeper grasp of complex subjects. AI tutors, offering real-time feedback and support, are becoming an essential part of the educational toolkit, complementing human teachers and enhancing the learning process. Yet, this technological infusion prompts important discussions about data privacy, equity, and the role of educators in an increasingly automated environment. As AI reshapes traditional educational paradigms, it beckons us to critically consider how best to harness its potential while ensuring an equitable and effective learning experience for all. This chapter delves into these concepts, exploring how AI is not only influencing the ways we learn but also challenging us to rethink education itself.

Adaptive Learning Technologies

As we delve into the transformative influence of AI in education, adaptive learning technologies emerge as a beacon of innovation, reshaping how students learn and teachers instruct. With the rapid advancement of artificial intelligence, these technologies have gained momentum, promising a more personalized and efficient educational journey. At the heart of adaptive learning lies the ability to adjust content and resources in real-time to cater to each student's unique learning pace and style.

Traditionally, education has followed a one-size-fits-all approach, where all students are expected to learn at the same pace using identical resources. This method often overlooks the diverse needs of students, some of whom may require additional time on certain topics, while others might benefit from more challenging material. Adaptive learning technologies address this gap by harnessing AI and data analytics to tailor the educational experience, enhancing both engagement and comprehension.

One of the core components of adaptive learning systems is their data-driven approach. These systems continuously gather and analyze data on each student's performance, identifying patterns, strengths, and weaknesses. This data is then used to modify the instructional path, ensuring that students receive the optimal level of challenge and support. For instance, if a student struggles with a particular math concept, the system might provide additional resources, such as video tutorials or practice exercises, until proficiency is achieved.

Moreover, adaptive learning technologies are not confined to any specific age group. From primary education to higher learning institutions, they have been implemented across various educational settings. In primary schools, adaptive learning helps in building foundational skills by making complex concepts accessible through interactive and engaging content. For college students, these technologies offer tools that aid in mastering specialized subjects, thus preparing them for their future careers.

The potential of adaptive learning extends beyond just enhancing individual student outcomes. When integrated effectively, these technologies can transform entire educational systems. By using adaptive learning platforms, schools and institutions can identify common learning trends and challenges faced by students. This enables educators to refine their teaching strategies and curricula to better serve the student body, creating a ripple effect of improvement throughout the educational ecosystem.

Despite their numerous advantages, the implementation of adaptive learning technologies is not without challenges. There are concerns over data privacy and the ethical use of student information, especially when it comes to safeguarding sensitive data. Educators and technology developers must work together to establish clear guidelines and protocols to ensure that data is handled responsibly. Additionally, the reliance on technology raises questions about accessibility, particularly in under-resourced schools that may lack the infrastructure to support such advanced systems.

An essential aspect of adaptive learning is the role of the teacher. Far from replacing educators, these technologies serve as powerful tools that can enhance teaching methods and free up valuable time. Teachers can leverage adaptive learning data to gain insights into student progress, allowing them to provide targeted interventions where necessary. This shift not only empowers educators but also fosters a more collaborative learning environment, where students feel supported and motivated.

Furthermore, the rise of adaptive learning technologies invites a paradigm shift in education itself. It encourages a more learner-centric approach, where the focus is not solely on rote memorization but on critical thinking, problem-solving, and lifelong learning skills. This is crucial in preparing students to navigate a rapidly changing world where adaptability and continuous learning are key to success.

As adaptive learning technologies continue to evolve, their potential to revolutionize education becomes increasingly apparent. The future may see these systems becoming more sophisticated, incorporating emerging AI techniques like deep learning and natural language processing to further enhance personalization. Envisioning a world where every student has an individualized learning path is no longer a distant dream but a tangible possibility, thanks to these innovative technologies.

In conclusion, adaptive learning technologies represent a significant stride toward democratizing education and making quality learning accessible to all. By tailoring the learning experience to individual needs, they hold the promise of unlocking the full potential of every learner. As educators, policymakers, and technologists collaborate to refine and expand these systems, we move closer to a future where education is not just about imparting knowledge but inspiring curiosity, creativity, and a lifelong love for learning.

AI Tutors and the Classroom

In classrooms worldwide, the presence of artificial intelligence is reshaping the traditional dynamics of teaching and learning. Once considered a distant vision, AI tutors are increasingly becoming a reality, offering personalized educational support that adapts to the unique needs of each student. The implications of AI in education are profound, altering not just how subjects are taught, but also how students engage with the material and one another.

AI tutors operate with the remarkable ability to personalize instruction. Traditional classrooms, with their one-size-fits-all approach, often struggle to meet the individual learning paces and styles of students. However, AI tutors leverage vast amounts of data and sophisticated algorithms to understand each student's strengths and weaknesses. This enables them to tailor lessons accordingly, ensuring that students who need extra help can focus on areas where they struggle, while those advancing more quickly can explore further challenges. This personalization fosters a learning environment where students are encouraged to excel at their own pace, reducing frustration and boosting confidence.

Moreover, AI tutors provide feedback that is immediate and specific. In a conventional classroom setting, the time teachers can dedicate to each student is limited, often leaving many without the comprehensive support they require. AI systems, on the other hand, analyze responses instantly, offering constructive feedback and allowing students to correct mistakes on the spot. This immediacy not only aids retention but also accelerates the learning process. Over time, students develop a more robust understanding of the material, and their improved competence reflects in their performance and enthusiasm for learning.

One notable aspect of AI tutors is their potential to remedy educational inequality. In many parts of the world, educational resources are scarce, and experienced teachers are a rarity. AI tutors can serve as a valuable supplement, bringing quality education to regions where students would otherwise have limited opportunities. By democratizing access to learning resources, AI holds the promise of leveling the educational playing field, granting students from diverse backgrounds the chance to succeed.

However, the introduction of AI tutors in classrooms comes with its set of challenges. One concern is the role of human educators in an AI-enhanced classroom. While AI can assist in delivering content and monitoring progress, it cannot replace the uniquely human skills that teachers bring to the table, such as empathy, inspiration, and the ability to foster interpersonal relationships. The challenge lies in integrating AI into the educational environment in a way that complements and enhances the teacher's role, rather than undermining or replacing it.

There is also the issue of data privacy and ethics. As AI tutors collect and analyze data to customize learning paths, the question of who owns this data and how it is protected becomes paramount.

Educational institutions and technology providers must ensure stringent data security measures are in place to safeguard student information. Moreover, ethical considerations regarding how data is used to influence learning pathways must be addressed transparently and responsibly.

Despite these challenges, the potential benefits of AI tutors in the classroom are extensive. By alleviating routine tasks, AI allows teachers to focus more on delivering creative and engaging lessons. This shift in focus can transform the learning experience, making it more interactive and less reliant on rote memorization. Furthermore, with AI handling some of the more tedious administrative responsibilities, teachers can concentrate on mentoring their students and fostering a supportive classroom environment.

AI tutors also open the door to new, innovative learning methods. By using data-driven insights, educators can experiment with flipped classrooms, gamified learning, and other modern educational strategies that might not have been feasible in the past. These approaches can make learning more enjoyable and interactive, appealing to a generation that is comfortable with technology and accustomed to instant feedback and results.

Ultimately, the success of AI tutors in classrooms hinges on a balanced approach. Educational stakeholders—from policymakers to teachers, parents, and students—must be involved in ongoing dialogues about how best to integrate AI technologies. Collaborative efforts are essential to ensure that AI tools are developed and utilized in ways that respect educational values and support diverse learning needs.

As we look toward the future, the integration of AI tutors promises to transform the educational landscape in ways we are only beginning to understand. By empowering educators and engaging students with tailored and immersive learning experiences, AI has the potential to make education more accessible, effective, and enriching than ever before. However, vigilance is necessary to ensure that this powerful technology is harnessed ethically, responsibly, and creatively, so that it can contribute positively to the next generation of learners.

Chapter 8:
Ethics of AI

The rapid growth of artificial intelligence introduces profound ethical challenges that we must confront in our increasingly digitized world. While AI systems hold the promise of efficiency and remarkable innovation, they also navigate a minefield of ethical concerns, primarily surrounding privacy and decision-making. Imagine a world where data is both the fuel and the fire—a catalyst for growth yet a potential threat when privacy becomes a commodity to be traded. The ethical landscape is further complicated when AI begins making decisions that impact lives and industries. Who bears responsibility for these automated choices? The creators, the users, or the algorithms themselves? As we forge ahead, understanding these ethical dimensions empowers us to harness AI responsibly, ensuring technology serves humanity without compromising fundamental values. This exploration isn't merely academic; it demands a societal reckoning that aligns advancing technologies with our shared moral compass.

Privacy Concerns with AI

Artificial Intelligence (AI) has woven itself into the fabric of our daily lives, offering astounding capabilities and conveniences. Yet, with this integration comes the pressing concern of privacy. The more AI systems connect with our personal devices and tap into vast pools of data, the greater the potential for misuse and intrusion. The trade-off between convenience and privacy is a delicate balance, and it's a concern that grows even more profound as these systems become more ubiquitous and sophisticated.

In recent years, data has emerged as the new currency of the digital age. AI systems, by their very nature, thrive on data. They are designed to learn and make predictions based on large datasets, which often include personal information. This rich store of data enables AI to anticipate user needs, personalize experiences, and even automate decision-making processes. However, the aggregation of such data raises significant privacy issues. Who controls this information? How is it stored, and for what purposes can it be used? The answers to these questions are often unclear, leading to uncertainties that threaten personal privacy.

One of the most striking examples of privacy concerns with AI is the proliferation of surveillance technologies. In cities around the world, AI-driven surveillance systems have been deployed to enhance security and monitor public spaces. While these technologies can improve safety, they also have the potential to infringe on individual privacy rights. Constant surveillance alters the very nature of privacy, eroding the sense of personal freedom and liberty in public domains. The nuances between necessary security measures and an overreach into personal space require careful oversight and transparent regulations.

Moreover, the rise of AI in personal devices, such as smartphones and home assistants, further highlights the privacy challenges. These devices are often equipped with voice recognition technology, always listening for commands. They're capable of collecting a massive amount of personal data, from voice patterns to behavioral habits, often without the user fully comprehending the extent of data collection. This constant surveillance in private spaces can feel invasive and may contribute to a broader anxiety about privacy dissolution.

The opaque nature of AI algorithms adds another layer of complexity to privacy concerns. Many AI systems operate as "black boxes," where inputs and outputs are visible, but the internal decision-making processes remain hidden. This lack of transparency makes it difficult for individuals to understand how their data is being used, which can lead to mistrust. Furthermore, when these systems make decisions on matters as personal as credit scoring or job applications, the stakes become even higher, amplifying calls for greater transparency and fairness.

Regulations like the General Data Protection Regulation (GDPR) in the European Union highlight efforts to address these privacy concerns. GDPR enforces strict guidelines on data protection and privacy, emphasizing user consent and data access rights. However, similar regulatory frameworks are not uniformly established across the globe. As AI technology transcends borders, the lack of consistent international standards complicates governance and enforcement, leaving many users vulnerable to privacy violations.

Another critical aspect of AI-related privacy concerns is data security. As AI systems interact with diverse datasets across various platforms, they become lucrative targets for cyberattacks. Breaches can lead to unauthorized access to sensitive information, which can be exploited for financial gain, identity theft, or other malicious purposes. As criminals become more sophisticated, the need for robust security measures is more pressing than ever, placing a significant responsibility on companies to protect user data effectively.

While the challenges are significant, there is hope in the potential solutions and advancements in privacy-preserving technologies. Techniques like differential privacy and federated learning offer promising approaches to maintaining user privacy. Differential privacy ensures that datasets can be used for analysis without exposing individual information, while federated learning enables AI to train models locally on devices instead of transferring raw data to central servers. These methods seek to balance the need for data utilization with the preservation of privacy.

Raising public awareness and educating users about privacy and AI is equally vital. As individuals become more informed about how AI systems operate and the kind of data they require, they can make more conscious decisions about their interaction with such technologies. Promoting digital literacy, especially around AI, empowers users to demand better safeguards and fosters a culture where privacy is treated with the importance it deserves.

Ultimately, addressing privacy concerns necessitates a collaborative effort involving policymakers, technologists, and society at large. Policymakers must establish frameworks that ensure responsible data use, encouraging innovation while protecting individual rights. Technologists are challenged to create systems that are not only advanced but also transparent and ethical. Society must engage in nuanced conversations about the value of privacy in an increasingly digital age, advocating for their rights and holding the stakeholders accountable.

The integration of AI into our lives brings both promise and peril. Navigating the privacy concerns associated with AI requires vigilance, adaptability, and an unwavering commitment to preserving individual freedoms in an era where data is king. Balancing technological progress with personal privacy is not just an ethical imperative but a societal one, demanding our collective involvement and ongoing dialogue.

Ethical Implications of Automated Decision-Making

Artificial intelligence and algorithms have woven themselves into the fabric of our lives, often operating behind the scenes in ways we're only beginning to comprehend. At the heart of this silent revolution is automated decision-making, a process where machines weigh options and decide based on data-driven algorithms. It might seem harmless or even beneficial, but as we peel back the layers, it becomes clear that this technological prowess is not without its ethical quandaries.

Consider the context of hiring new employees. Increasingly, companies are employing AI to sift through resumes and rank candidates. On the surface, this might look like an efficient way to streamline hiring and eliminate biases. However, automated systems can inadvertently perpetuate existing biases if the data they're trained on is skewed. For instance, if past hiring data reflects a preference for certain demographics, the AI might unknowingly continue to favor similar profiles, thus perpetuating systemic inequalities.

Another pressing concern is transparency. When decisions are made by AI, the rationale isn't always clear to those affected. For example, when a bank denies a loan application based on an algorithm's analysis, the applicant might not understand why they were rejected. Was it due to their credit history, income level, or another factor altogether? The lack of transparency can lead to frustration and a sense of injustice, as those impacted by these decisions have little recourse or understanding of the decision-making process.

Moreover, the rise of automated decision-making brings up questions about accountability. In traditional decision-making, individuals or organizations are held accountable for their actions. But when an AI makes a mistake—say, a wrongful denial of social services or a misdiagnosis in a medical context—who is to blame? The developer of the AI? The company that implemented it? As AI systems grow more complex, untangling the web of accountability becomes increasingly challenging.

Privacy issues further complicate the ethical landscape. Many automated decision-making systems require vast amounts of personal data to function effectively. This data must be collected, stored, and analyzed, often without the explicit consent of the individuals involved. Such practices can inadvertently lead to surveillance and exploitation of personal information. When these systems determine a person's eligibility for welfare, insurance premiums, or even parole, the stakes become incredibly high, and the individuals' privacy is often sacrificed at the altar of convenience.

In educational settings, automated decision-making can dictate a student's trajectory, from admissions processes to personalized learning tracks. While this can offer tailored education experiences, it risks pigeonholing students based on predictive assessments rather than potential. For example, if an algorithm predicts that a student isn't likely to excel in math, it might limit their exposure to advanced math classes, potentially stifling latent talent that might have thrived under different circumstances.

The implementation of AI systems in law enforcement and the criminal justice system also raises significant ethical concerns. Predictive policing tools, which use data to forecast where crimes might occur or identify potential suspects, have been criticized for reinforcing racial biases that exist within the dataset. When automated decisions impact liberty and safety, the consequences of ethical oversights can be dire and widespread, often disproportionately affecting marginalized communities.

Consumer markets are heavily influenced by automated decision-making, impacting everything from the advertisements we see to the products recommended on our shopping sites. While this can enhance user experience by providing relevant content, it also raises questions about manipulation and autonomy. Are our choices truly our own when algorithms subtly nudge us toward certain products or ideologies based on past behaviors?

There's also the notion of informed consent in a world dominated by AI. As algorithms increasingly mediate our choices and interactions, do individuals genuinely understand and agree to how their data is used? Often, people inadvertently yield their data rights through lengthy user agreements filled with legal jargon. Without clear understanding and consent, the ethical grounds of data-driven decision-making become shaky.

Despite these ethical challenges, automated decision-making does offer tremendous potential. It has the capacity to drive efficiency, discover insights, and handle complex problems at a scale unimaginable for humans alone. For instance, AI's ability to analyze vast datasets can lead to breakthroughs in healthcare diagnostics, potentially saving lives through early detection of diseases. To harness such benefits while mitigating ethical risks, a balanced approach is crucial.

One potential solution lies in developing robust ethical guidelines and regulatory frameworks that promote accountability, transparency, and fairness. Developers should incorporate ethical considerations throughout the AI development process, ensuring that systems are designed and tested for bias and discrimination. Moreover, there should be avenues for human oversight and recourse in automated decision-making processes.

Education and public awareness are equally important. As society becomes more reliant on automated systems, individuals need to understand not only how these technologies work but also the ethical questions they raise. This understanding empowers people to advocate for fair and transparent AI policies that align with shared values and rights.

Ultimately, navigating the ethical implications of automated decision-making requires a collaborative effort, involving technologists, policymakers, ethicists, and the public. By approaching AI with a critical and informed mindset, we can strive to craft a future where technology acts as a force for equity and positive change, rather than an unchecked force that deepens social divides.

Chapter 9:
AI and the Economy

As artificial intelligence continues to weave itself into the very fabric of our economic systems, it's reshaping industries and redefining what work means. No longer bound by the limitations of human labor alone, economics are witnessing a seismic shift, brimming with both potential and pitfalls. On the one hand, AI has the capability to boost productivity and spur economic growth by driving efficiencies and unlocking new markets. Yet, this technological renaissance also poses significant challenges, such as widespread job displacement and the widening gap between skilled and unskilled workers. Businesses face a balancing act of maximizing AI's economic advantages while mitigating its societal impacts. This transformation calls for a nuanced approach, where government, industry, and individuals collaborate to harness AI's power for an inclusive future. As we navigate this economic metamorphosis, the stakes are high, but so too are the opportunities for innovation and prosperity.

The Impact on Job Markets

Artificial intelligence and its transformative power are reshaping the global job market at an unprecedented pace. This seismic shift is as fascinating as it is unsettling, given its ability to radically alter traditional employment landscapes. Much like the industrial revolutions of the past, AI heralds both innovation and disruption, bringing with it both opportunities and challenges that require careful navigation.

To appreciate the impact of AI on job markets, it's crucial to understand the duality of its effects: job displacement and job creation. AI's proficiency in executing repetitive tasks with unmatched speed and precision means that certain jobs, particularly those tied to routine and predictable activities, are increasingly at risk. Industries such as manufacturing, customer service, and data entry are observing automation supplant roles traditionally filled by humans. Yet, while machines are replacing some jobs, they are also creating new ones, particularly in sectors that demand creativity, interpersonal skills, and advanced technical expertise.

The spectrum of jobs most susceptible to AI automation generally includes roles with high levels of routine. Consider an assembly line worker whose tasks involve standardized processes. Here, AI systems excel at executing the same task with unfaltering accuracy and no requirement for breaks. But automation isn't exclusive to blue-collar occupations. White-collar roles in fields like accounting or legal research are also being reshaped as AI algorithms analyze data more efficiently than a human mind ever could.

Conversely, the potential for job creation is immense. AI has the power to unleash a wave of opportunities in tech-related fields, ranging from AI ethics specialists to advanced data scientists. These roles demand skills unique to our technologically advanced era. However, seizing these opportunities requires significant reskilling and upskilling efforts. Lifelong learning and adaptability become indispensable tools for the workforce to transition into the demands of the AI economy.

Moreover, AI is nurturing an ecosystem where human creativity is increasingly valued. Consider the role of AI in augmenting human capabilities; AI tools help unlock creative potential, opening new frontiers in art, design, and beyond. Jobs that involve strategic decision-making, emotional intelligence, and creative problem-solving are less likely to be automated, thereby increasing their significance in the AI-driven job market.

On a broader scale, AI's impact varies across different economies and regions. In some emerging markets, the integration of AI could leapfrog infrastructure gaps, potentially accelerating economic growth and speeding up the development of new industries. However, in areas dependent on low-skill labor, AI could exacerbate existing inequalities, creating a divide that policymakers must address with urgency.

The ripple effects of AI on employment extend beyond economic statistics; they pierce the social fabric of societies. The potential for increased unemployment and job transition discomfort can lead to social unrest and economic instability if not managed prudently. Thus, governments, industries, and educational institutions must collaborate to mitigate such risks through tailored policies and programs.

Education systems worldwide must be reimagined to align more closely with the skillsets demanded by AI-enhanced economies. Curricula that integrate STEM education with critical thinking, creativity, and ethical insights into technology will empower the future workforce to thrive alongside AI. Continuous professional development programs and collaborative industry-academic partnerships can offer pathways for professionals to reskill efficiently.

The rise of AI also presents a critical opportunity to reevaluate work's nature and its role in human lives. As automation handles mundane tasks, there's potential for a paradigm shift towards more meaningful, fulfilling work. A societal rethinking about work-life balance could lead to innovative labor practices, including shorter workweeks and increased focus on well-being.

However, embracing AI's full potential requires a nuanced understanding of its limitations and ethical considerations.

Transparency in AI decision-making processes, bias mitigation strategies, and robust privacy protections should be integral components of any AI implementation strategy. Trust in AI systems is paramount, as their influence becomes more pervasive in job markets and daily life.

Overall, AI promises to redefine the very essence of work. While its journey promises challenges, it equally promises a horizon filled with unprecedented opportunities. By fostering adaptability, encouraging innovative educational practices, and embedding ethical considerations in AI development, societies can navigate this transformative journey thoughtfully. In doing so, we may not just encounter a future where AI augments our capabilities but shapes a landscape where human potential finds new and extraordinary ways to thrive.

Economic Benefits and Challenges

Artificial intelligence (AI) stands at the forefront of technological advancement, with its potential to revolutionize the global economy extensively documented. As it weaves itself into various economic sectors, AI promises substantial benefits ranging from productivity enhancements to new streams of revenue. Yet, with these benefits also come significant challenges that could reshape economic structures as we know them.

One of the most compelling economic advantages of AI is its potential to significantly boost productivity. By automating routine tasks, AI enables businesses to operate more efficiently and with greater precision. Companies across industries—from manufacturing to retail—are already experiencing productivity gains as AI handles everything from quality control in factories to inventory management in warehouses. This increased efficiency can reduce operating costs, allowing businesses to reinvest savings into innovation, further driving economic growth.

Moreover, AI's ability to analyze vast amounts of data rapidly and accurately holds immense economic promise. It empowers companies to make informed decisions with unprecedented speed, fostering a dynamic business environment that is responsive to real-time changes. For example, AI algorithms in financial services predict market trends, helping investors mitigate risks and maximize returns. Such applications have the potential to stimulate economic activity by optimizing investment strategies and promoting stability in volatile markets.

Additionally, AI's role in fostering new industries cannot be overstated. As AI technologies mature, they are expected to spawn entirely new sectors and job categories. From AI-driven pharmaceutical research unlocking faster drug discovery to autonomous vehicles creating a ripple effect in transportation, AI is forecasted to open avenues for economic development that were previously unimaginable. These innovations could not only generate new revenue streams but also redefine traditional business models, challenging companies to adapt and innovate continually.

However, the economic changes ushered in by AI are not without their challenges. One of the most pressing issues is its impact on job markets. As AI systems become more capable, they will inevitably automate a wide range of tasks currently performed by humans. While some argue that AI will create more jobs than it displaces, there's considerable uncertainty about the types of jobs that will emerge and whether they will match the skillsets of the displaced workers. This potential mismatch could exacerbate economic inequality, disproportionately affecting lower-skilled workers and widening the gap between different socioeconomic groups.

Moreover, the implementation of AI requires substantial investment, which poses a challenge for smaller businesses and developing nations that may not have the resources to compete with larger, more established entities. This disparity in AI adoption could lead to a digital divide where economic benefits are concentrated among a few players, leaving others at a disadvantage. Consequently, it becomes imperative for policymakers to consider how to make AI development inclusive and equitable, ensuring that its benefits reach all strata of society.

Regulatory challenges also loom large in the adoption of AI within the economy. As AI technologies evolve rapidly, maintaining appropriate oversight and ensuring they operate within ethical frameworks becomes increasingly complex. Ensuring data privacy, preventing algorithmic biases, and safeguarding against unintended consequences are critical issues that require comprehensive regulatory approaches. Governments and international bodies need to collaborate to develop frameworks that not only foster innovation but also protect public interest.

Furthermore, the economic integration of AI poses ethical considerations that cannot be ignored. The creation and deployment of AI systems are often guided by commercial interests, which may not always align with broader societal values. There is a risk that in pursuit of economic gains, societal norms and ethical standards could be compromised. As such, balancing economic benefits with ethical imperatives will be a significant challenge for both businesses and policymakers as they navigate this AI-driven landscape.

Despite these challenges, the economic benefits of AI present a transformative opportunity. By fostering an environment that supports innovation while addressing the associated challenges, societies can harness AI's potential to drive sustainable economic growth. This requires a concerted effort from governments, industries, and communities to create an ecosystem that not only encourages technological advancement but also ensures that the resulting economic benefits are distributed equitably.

In conclusion, AI holds the potential to redefine the economic landscape in profound ways. While its benefits in productivity, decision-making, and industry creation are immense, the challenges it presents are equally formidable. Addressing these challenges will require nuanced and forward-thinking strategies to ensure that AI contributes positively to global economic well-being. As we continue down this path, a balanced approach that embraces innovation while safeguarding against potential pitfalls will be crucial to maximizing AI's economic potential.

Chapter 10:
Autonomous Vehicles

As we delve into the realm of autonomous vehicles, we're stepping into a world once confined to the imaginations of science fiction. The roads are transforming as self-driving cars promise to redefine the very notion of transportation. At the heart of these vehicles lies a sophisticated amalgamation of sensors, cameras, and artificial intelligence that navigate us safely from point A to point B. The potential ripple effects are enormous: reduced traffic congestion, lower emissions, and increased accessibility for those unable to drive. Yet, these advancements raise critical questions about safety, regulation, and the future of our cities. In understanding these driverless vehicles, we're not merely exploring technological innovation; we're examining a profound shift in our relationship with machines and our environment. The journey of autonomous vehicles is not just about overcoming technical hurdles but also about navigating the ethical, social, and economic landscapes they disrupt.

Technology Behind Self-Driving Cars

The advent of autonomous vehicles represents one of the most fascinating technological advancements of the 21st century. At its core, a self-driving car is a masterpiece of interconnected systems and sophisticated technologies working harmoniously to navigate the complexities of the real world without human intervention. These vehicles are engineered to perceive, analyze, and respond to their environment in a manner that mimics human driving but with the potential for enhanced safety and efficiency.

A pivotal component of self-driving car technology is the sensor suite, which serves as the vehicle's sensory organs. These sensors collect vast streams of data from the car's surroundings, allowing it to make informed decisions with precision. Lidar (Light Detection and Ranging) is particularly crucial as it constructs a detailed, three-dimensional image of the environment using laser beams. This sensor helps in identifying objects, measuring distances accurately, and determining the shape and size of obstacles. Meanwhile, radar sensors enhance this capability by detecting the speed and direction of other vehicles, even in adverse weather conditions.

Vision is another critical aspect, and here, cameras play a significant role. These optical devices capture visual information similar to how humans use their eyes, providing color and perspective. Cameras enable the vehicle to recognize road signs, lane markings, pedestrians, and cyclists. Unlike lidar and radar, which offer structural insights, cameras provide contextual understanding. Integrating data from these diverse sensors through sensor fusion allows self-driving cars to maintain situational awareness and adapt to dynamic driving conditions.

However, sensing is just one piece of a much larger puzzle. The collected data must be processed and interpreted, a task undertaken by advanced machine learning algorithms and artificial intelligence. At the center of this processing is the vehicle's brain—a powerful onboard computer equipped with neural networks trained to recognize and interpret complex patterns. These networks learn from countless scenarios, enabling the car to predict the actions of other road users and to take preemptive measures accordingly.

Deep learning, a subset of machine learning, plays a particularly critical role in processing the immense amounts of data collected by sensors. By mimicking the functions of the human brain, deep learning algorithms learn from extensive datasets composed of real-world driving situations, honing their ability to recognize traffic signals, detect obstacles, and make split-second decisions. This capability is a vital aspect of ensuring the vehicle's performance and safety meet rigorous standards.

Beyond perception and analysis, decision-making is another cornerstone of self-driving technology. An autonomous vehicle must make countless decisions every second—from navigating complex intersections to adjusting speed based on traffic flow. This decision-making process is powered by sophisticated algorithms that integrate the vehicle's sensory inputs with pre-programmed knowledge of traffic laws and road etiquette. These algorithms are designed to prioritize safety, ensuring a careful and defensive approach to driving while efficiently progressing toward destinations.

Moreover, connectivity augments the capabilities of autonomous vehicles. Through vehicle-to-vehicle (V2V) and vehicle-to-infrastructure (V2I) communication, self-driving cars access real-time data about traffic conditions, upcoming hazards, and optimal routing information. This interconnected communication enables vehicles to anticipate changes in traffic patterns and share immediate updates, significantly enhancing traffic safety and reducing congestion.

Despite the incredible advancements in autonomous vehicle technology, development and implementation aren't devoid of challenges. A significant issue is achieving a level of safety and reliability that meets or exceeds human-driven vehicles. AI models must be fine-tuned to handle rare and unpredictable events—often referred to as edge cases—that human drivers might encounter infrequently. Additionally, the ethical considerations that arise when programming these vehicles to make decisions in critical situations are hotly debated. Should a vehicle prioritize the safety of its passengers, pedestrians, or other drivers in an unavoidable collision scenario? These ethical algorithms are pivotal in engendering societal trust in autonomous technology.

Regulatory challenges also accompany technological advancements in self-driving vehicles. Laws and guidelines governing autonomous cars are still evolving as nations grapple with safety standards, liability issues, and insurance implications. Establishing a comprehensive legal framework that provides clarity and assurance for manufacturers, consumers, and third parties is crucial for the widespread adoption of these vehicles.

Furthermore, the computational power required for full autonomy continues to push the boundaries of current technology. Processing vast amounts of data in real-time necessitates immense computing capabilities and energy efficiency. Tech companies continually innovate in hardware design, exploring advanced chip architectures and energy-efficient systems to meet these demands.

Looking ahead, the future of self-driving cars promises a transportation revolution that could redefine personal mobility, reduce road accidents, and decrease traffic congestion. As these technologies evolve, collaboration between technology developers, policymakers, and the public becomes essential to building an autonomous future that aligns with societal values and expectations.

In summary, the technology behind self-driving cars is a marvel of modern engineering, combining sophisticated sensor arrays, advanced AI, and robust communication systems. Although challenges remain, continued advancements hold the promise of transforming how we move, making transportation safer and more accessible for everyone. Autonomous vehicles represent not just a technological achievement but a leap toward a future where unimaginable possibilities become reality.

AI and Transportation Safety

The promise of autonomous vehicles isn't just about leisurely rides without the need of human control. It's a profound leap towards reshaping the very core of transportation safety. Currently, human error accounts for a staggering proportion of road accidents, and AI-driven vehicles have the potential to mitigate these errors significantly. But how is this transformation poised to unfold, and what challenges does it bring?

One of the foundational elements of AI's role in transportation safety is its ability to process immense amounts of data in real-time. This processing power allows self-driving systems to detect obstacles, make split-second decisions, and adjust to dynamic environments far more efficiently than a human ever could. Advanced cameras, sensors, and radar systems provide these vehicles with a 360-degree awareness that no human driver would be capable of sustaining.

While technology brings solutions, it also creates its own set of challenges. One such challenge is ensuring the reliability and accuracy of these data streams. Imagine the multitude of scenarios an autonomous vehicle might encounter: a pedestrian unexpectedly crossing, sudden weather changes, or even encountering law enforcement directions. Each scenario requires precise decision-making, for which AI systems must be painstakingly trained through countless simulations and real-world learning experiences.

Furthermore, the software that powers these systems needs to be foolproof. There's little room for bugs or unexpected behavior when lives are at stake. Companies developing autonomous technology, therefore, prioritize extensive testing phases, involving millions of miles driven on both simulated and actual roads. Yet, with all this preparation, there remain questions about how these systems respond in the face of ethical dilemmas. Who determines the course of action when an accident seems unavoidable? The programming choices made by developers can carry significant ethical implications.

Beyond technology, the regulatory landscape presents another layer of complexity. Various countries and states are evolving their laws to adapt to the presence of self-driving cars on their roads. Such regulations have to balance innovation with public safety, ensuring that any rollout of autonomous vehicles doesn't outpace the establishment of comprehensive safety standards. Policymakers need to work collaboratively with technologists, engineers, and ethicists to create frameworks that allow for both advancement and assurance of public welfare.

In parallel, there is a societal aspect that cannot be ignored. Public perception of autonomous vehicles significantly impacts their adoption. Trust plays a crucial role, and building this trust involves transparency about how AI decisions are made within these vehicles, as well as clear communication about the safety data. Education campaigns that inform the public about the benefits and limitations of self-driving technology might pave the way for greater acceptance and understanding.

Despite these hurdles, the potential benefits of AI in transportation safety are transformative. Autonomous vehicles could reduce traffic congestion by optimizing driving patterns and decreasing unnecessary stops and starts. This efficiency, coupled with the reduction in accidents, could lead to lower insurance costs and healthcare expenses related to road traffic injuries. Emergency services could be redirected away from accident scenes, conserving resources for critical caregiving.

The urban landscape, too, stands to change. The need for extensive parking areas could diminish, giving way to more green spaces and pedestrian-friendly zones. People living in cities may eventually move towards shared autonomous vehicle models, reducing the number of unoccupied cars at any given moment.

However, as AI continues to advance, the intersection between technological capability and transportation safety will remain a topic of intense research and discussion. AI models have to be robust against software attacks and glitches that could compromise safety. As we explore the role of AI in transportation safety, we must remain vigilant about the ethical implications and societal impacts.

In conclusion, AI's integration into transportation signifies more than just a technological upgrade; it represents an evolution in our approach to safety, efficiency, and urban planning. Autonomous vehicles symbolize a frontier where technology meets everyday life, bringing challenges but promising rewards that could redefine our transportation ecosystem for generations to come. The road to fully autonomous and safe transportation is still under construction, but the foundations being laid today carry the potential for a safer tomorrow.

Chapter 11:
The Future of AI

As we look toward the horizon of artificial intelligence, it's clear that the trajectory of AI development will be both transformative and unpredictable. The advancing capabilities of AI hint at a future where automation could seamlessly integrate into our daily lives, revolutionizing industries from healthcare to transportation. Nevertheless, as AI continues to evolve, it's crucial to consider the societal impact, including potential job displacement and ethical considerations. There's optimism that AI could solve many pressing global challenges, but there's also an underlying caution about the implications of such powerful technology. Navigating this future demands a balance between innovation and responsibility, ensuring that AI serves humanity rather than dominates it. In this unfolding narrative, the role of comprehensive policy-making and public engagement will be essential to harness AI's potential for the greater good while mitigating its risks.

Predicting AI Trends

As we gaze into the shimmering horizon of technological advancement, predicting AI trends feels much like predicting the weather—while the big patterns are visible, the smaller details remain elusive. The intersection of artificial intelligence and society exists as a dynamic juncture where possibilities abound but are tempered by unpredictable elements such as policy changes, technological breakthroughs, and social acceptance. Still, analyzing current trajectories can provide a window into where AI might take us next.

In the immediate future, one of the most transformative trends is the maturation of AI models that seamlessly integrate into our daily lives. Take, for example, language models and their rapidly evolving capabilities. Not only are they becoming more adept at understanding and generating human-like text, but they are also increasingly nuanced in offering context-aware solutions, which has vast implications for personal and professional communication. This evolution will likely continue to deepen, blurring the lines between human and AI interactions in unprecedented ways.

Beyond just conversation, AI's role in decision-making is becoming more autonomous. We see this in sectors where AI has made significant inroads, such as finance and healthcare. Algorithms that learn from patterns and predict outcomes are being entrusted with more decisions traditionally made by humans. The key trend here is the shift from AI as an assistant to AI as a trusted advisor, which raises questions about accountability and reliability, reinforcing the need for ethical frameworks.

Meanwhile, neural networks are set to grow even more complex and capable. The rise of deep learning architectures, particularly transformers, suggests a trajectory toward AI systems that can understand and interpret multifaceted inputs. These might range from multi-modal analysis—capturing and processing data from text, images, and audio simultaneously—to simulating real-world environments with a degree of accuracy previously thought unattainable. Further integration of such systems could dramatically impact fields like simulation-based training and virtual reality experiences.

As AI becomes more advanced, the infrastructure supporting these systems must evolve too. This trend points to an increased need for robust and scalable data ecosystems. With the exponential growth of data, AI techniques such as federated learning and edge computing are emerging as potential solutions to efficiently manage and process data. This reduces the dependency on central cloud services, paving the way for faster and more private AI solutions deployed directly on user devices.

AI is also increasingly central to tackling complex global issues, prominently climate change. Predictive analytics and AI-driven models are being used to understand environmental patterns and provide actionable insights for sustainability. In the years to come, this capability is expected to expand, as tools for predicting weather events, optimizing energy use, and managing natural resources improve, prompting a more sustainable interaction between human advancement and environmental stewardship.

As AI continues to permeate various sectors, it's crucial to anticipate shifts in workforce dynamics. Job transformation rather than elimination is the trend—where AI automates repetitive tasks, it also creates new roles focused on managing, training, and collaborating with AI systems. This could usher in an era of reskilling and upskilling, as workers adapt to new relationships with AI, highlighting the importance of educational systems re-engineering to address these emerging needs.

AI's penetration across global markets also demands a nuanced understanding of regional trends. We are witnessing varied approaches to AI integration—where some nations focus on aggressive commercialization, others prioritize regulatory frameworks to safeguard against potential risks. Therefore, international cooperation and policy alignment become essential to manage the global flow of AI technologies and standards, potentially leading to a new era of digital diplomacy.

Another significant trend is the burgeoning role of AI in creative fields. Algorithms that aid in music composition, art generation, and content curation are on the rise, pushing the boundaries of what machines can create. This only opens exciting avenues for collaboration between human creativity and machine intelligence, challenging our conventional notions of authorship and originality.

In security, AI is gearing up to play a dual role—both as a guardian and a potential adversary. Enhancements in AI-driven cybersecurity solutions aim to protect critical infrastructure against emerging threats. However, the same AI capabilities can be exploited maliciously, necessitating proactive defense strategies and ethical standards to ensure AI's benefits outweigh its risks.

Finally, as AI becomes more ubiquitous, questions about ethical AI implementation gather momentum. Society must grapple with issues related to bias, fairness, and transparency in algorithms. The crucial trend here is developing and adopting guidelines that not only embed ethical considerations into AI development but also ensure accountability in its deployment, fostering public trust and acceptance.

In conclusion, while none can predict the exact course AI will take, identifying these prevailing trends offers a glimpse into a future teeming with potential. We stand at the cusp of a transformative era, where AI promises to redefine the contours of human experience and knowledge. How we navigate these predictions—through innovation, governance, and education—will ultimately shape the future of artificial intelligence.

Long-Term Implications for Society

The future of artificial intelligence (AI) holds immense potential, but it brings with it a host of long-term implications for society that demand attention and foresight. As AI continues to evolve, its impact on various facets of our lives will only become more pronounced. These changes can touch everything from economic dynamics to the very nature of human relationships. The way societies choose to navigate this new landscape could define the balance between opportunity and challenge in the world of tomorrow.

At the heart of AI's potential lies the transformation of the job market. Automation and AI technologies could drastically change the nature of work, displacing certain jobs while creating new ones. On one hand, AI might relieve humans of monotonous tasks, freeing them to pursue more creative and meaningful careers. On the other, there's a real risk that the speed and scope of technological change could leave many without adequate livelihoods if systems fail to adapt. Society must proactively engage with these potential shifts, investing in education and retraining programs to mitigate potential fallout.

Moreover, AI's integration into decision-making processes raises ethical considerations surrounding accountability and transparency. Algorithms could increasingly mediate critical decisions in areas like finance, healthcare, and justice, affecting lives in significant ways. The black-box nature of many AI systems, where decision logic is opaque even to their creators, presents a conundrum. Ensuring these systems operate fairly and justly will require rigorous oversight and potentially new legal frameworks. Societal trust in AI will depend on these safeguards being robust and reliable.

Then, there's the matter of bias in artificial intelligence. AI systems trained on datasets that reflect societal biases might perpetuate or even exacerbate these prejudices. If left unchecked, this could deepen social inequalities. Addressing this challenge calls for a concerted effort in developing ethical AI practices and inclusive datasets. Researchers, policymakers, and technologists must work together to develop guidelines ensuring AI promotes equity rather than division.

The societal implications of AI stretch far into our personal lives, reshaping notions of privacy in an interconnected digital ecosystem. The pervasive deployment of AI technologies, from facial recognition to data-driven personalization, poses significant privacy risks. Users often trade personal data for convenience, sometimes without a full understanding of potential risks. Protecting individual privacy while harnessing AI's benefits will require careful consideration and possibly new regulatory frameworks that give people more control over their personal information.

Another pressing concern is AI's potential to enhance surveillance capabilities. While governments and companies argue that enhanced surveillance serves public safety, critics warn of its potential misuse. Surveillance powered by AI can lead to a society where privacy is virtually nonexistent, empowering authoritarian regimes or creating a surveillance state. Balancing privacy and security concerns will be a critical issue requiring delicate diplomacy and robust legal standards.

Moreover, AI's role in exchanging information has profound implications for democracy and public discourse. The capacity of AI technologies to influence perspectives through targeted advertisements and personalized content could undermine truthful dialogue and promote polarization. In the broader context, social media platforms, amplified by AI algorithms, have been associated with the spread of misinformation. It's imperative to strike a balance between technological innovation and the preservation of democratic ideals. Adequate safeguards and policies can enhance the accountability of AI-assisted platforms.

The environmental footprint of AI cannot be overlooked either. The computational power required for training large-scale AI models can be significant, posing additional concerns related to energy consumption and environmental sustainability. As AI becomes more integral to our global infrastructure, innovations in energy-efficient algorithms and sustainable practices must keep pace. Aligning AI development with ecological responsibility can ensure the technology contributes positively to global sustainability goals.

Additionally, AI's impact on human interaction is worth considering. As AI assumes roles traditionally filled by humans—whether as customer service assistants, tutors, or even companions—the quality and depth of human relationships could be altered. With AI's increasing presence in everyday life, there's a risk of societal fragmentation should individuals opt for digital interaction over face-to-face communication. Encouraging responsible and balanced AI use can help foster more meaningful relationships and ensure technology complements rather than replaces human connection.

As we navigate these implications, international cooperation will prove vital. AI is boundless, crossing borders with ease, which necessitates a coordinated global approach to addressing shared challenges. From establishing international norms and ethical standards to collaborating on AI governance, countries must engage in dialogue and partnerships to steer AI development responsibly. Such efforts could prevent technology from becoming a tool for economic dominance or geopolitical strife.

It's clear that AI will shape the trajectory of human progress, demanding vigilance and adaptability. While the long-term implications of AI pose daunting challenges, they also offer unprecedented opportunities to enhance societal well-being. By aligning AI's development with ethical and sustainable practices, humanity can harness its power to build a future where technology uplifts rather than divides. Only through mindful integration of AI into societal frameworks can we achieve a harmonious balance between the digital age's promises and perils.

Chapter 12:
AI in Creative Industries

In recent years, artificial intelligence has not only entered the technical realms of society but has made significant strides in creative industries as well, pushing the boundaries of art and entertainment. This convergence of technology and creativity has opened new pathways for artists and creators, offering them tools that expand their imagination and productivity. AI programs capable of generating stunning visual art, composing music, and even crafting scripts are changing the creative process itself, inviting humans to collaborate with machines in unprecedented ways. While purists may express concern over the influence of algorithms, suggesting a potential threat to human originality, many artists embrace AI as an empowering tool that enhances their craft. By suggesting novel ideas and patterns, AI serves as a co-creator that inspires innovation. As AI continues to evolve, it holds the promise of democratizing creativity, making artistic expression more accessible to people who might previously have lacked the technical skills, thus gradually reshaping the cultural landscape for the better.

AI and Art Generation

Art, in its myriad forms, has always functioned as a profound representation of human experience, encapsulating emotions, conveying ideas, and challenging perceptions. With the advent of artificial intelligence, a radical transformation is underway in the realm of art generation, ushering in a new era where creativity is not solely the preserve of humanity. AI artists, often indistinguishable from human creators, are contributing works that surprise and captivate audiences around the world. This fusion of technology and artistry not only expands the creative possibilities but also raises intriguing questions about authorship, authenticity, and the definition of art itself.

The process of generating art with AI involves complex algorithms trained on vast datasets of pre-existing artworks. These programs can create images, sculptures, and even music, using sophisticated artificial neural networks like Generative Adversarial Networks (GANs). With GANs, two neural networks work in tandem: one creates new outputs while the other evaluates them, pushing the system to produce increasingly refined artistic expressions. The outcomes are not mere copies but innovative renditions, perhaps akin to how a human artist might be inspired by those who have come before. This raises the tantalizing possibility of AI as a collaborator rather than just a tool.

While traditionalists may argue that creativity is an inherently human trait, AI has proved capable of mimicking, and sometimes seemingly transcending, human creativity. However, this also poses a philosophical conundrum: is art still art if created by a machine? The debate centers around the role of intention and emotion in art—elements AI lacks. Yet, others posit that AI could serve as a new medium, expanding the horizons of what is creatively possible and enabling artists to push the boundaries of imagination.

Compelling examples of AI-generated art have already entered mainstream consciousness. The sale of "Edmond de Belamy," an AI-created portrait, by Christie's auction house for $432,500 in 2018 marked a significant milestone. This event not only spotlighted AI's potential in the art market but also sparked a conversation on the value and impact of AI-presence in art. This painting serves as a harbinger of the potential cultural shifts AI art may incite, as collectors, critics, and the general public grapple with the integration of AI in the creative landscape.

AI's impact on art isn't confined to visual arts alone. In literature, for example, programs like OpenAI's GPT-3 are capable of writing poetry, stories, and even journalism. Musicians are using AI-based tools to compose new pieces, generating harmonious symphonies and novel soundscapes that merge human intuition with algorithmic precision. In filmmaking, AI is used for scriptwriting and editing, challenging traditional roles and functions in the creative process. These advances not only contribute to innovative outputs but also democratize art creation, permitting individuals without traditional skills to participate in creative processes.

Despite these advancements, AI-generated art is not without its criticisms and concerns. There is an ongoing debate about the originality of AI-generated works, especially when they heavily rely on pre-existing datasets. Questions about intellectual property and copyright infringement loom large when AI systems are trained on artworks without explicit consent from their creators. Furthermore, the proliferation of AI-generated content could potentially disrupt the livelihoods of human artists, creating a cultural economy that favors machines over people—a poignant reflection of the broader societal shifts AI brings.

As AI continues to evolve, the potential for deeply personalized art becomes more feasible. Imagine a world where AI creates art tailored to your moods, preferences, nuanced emotions, or even significant life moments. Using biometric data, AI could craft art that resonates on an individual level, transforming not only the consumption but the conception of art into a highly personal experience. This personalization could redefine the very nature of art, making it an interactive, living process rather than a static exhibition.

In educational settings, AI art generation can foster an innovative approach to learning, where students explore creativity through technology, learning not only about art but about the underlying algorithms that drive these systems. By integrating AI in arts education, learners can develop a deeper understanding of both art and technology, bridging an important gap and preparing them for a future where both are deeply interconnected.

Ultimately, AI and art generation represent a frontier where the human and the digital converge to form a new landscape of possibility. This convergence provides a unique laboratory for testing the limits of AI capabilities and offers a platform for dialogue about our relationship with technology. As AI systems become more integral in artistic creation, society will need to continually reflect on the implications: What does it mean to be an artist in the AI age? How do we define creativity? And how do these creations reflect and affect our humanity?

By embracing AI as a component of the creative process, we can learn to appreciate the symbiosis between human imagination and machine learning. As with any technological advancement, the key lies not in resisting change but in understanding and harnessing it. The art of the future is not solely about the materials and techniques of today, but about embracing the radical potential of what could be—ushered in by the combined creative forces of human and machine.

Music and Movie Recommendations

The world of music and movies has been revolutionized by artificial intelligence (AI) in recent years, fundamentally altering how we discover and consume entertainment. One of the most profound shifts has been in the way algorithms cater to our tastes, serving up personalized recommendations that feel almost clairvoyant in their accuracy. This transformation didn't happen overnight. Behind the scenes, a sophisticated interplay of data science and machine learning powers seemingly simple suggestions. As we delve into this topic, it's crucial to unravel just how these algorithms influence not only individual experiences but also the broader creative landscape.

At the heart of music and movie recommendation systems is the intent to predict what you'll enjoy next based on your past behaviors and similar user profiles. Services like Spotify and Netflix have mastered this art. They utilize a blend of collaborative filtering, content-based filtering, and increasingly, deep learning techniques. Collaborative filtering works by analyzing user interactions, identifying patterns, and suggesting content liked by users with similar tastes. Content-based filtering, on the other hand, focuses on the intrinsic features of the items themselves, such as genre, artists, or themes.

Deep learning, with its ability to process vast amounts of complex data, has further refined these systems. Neural networks can assess the subtle nuances and multifaceted layers of artistic works, understanding not just the categorization of content but also the emotional and contextual dimensions that make music and movies unique to each listener or viewer. This enables platforms to offer recommendations that are not only precise but also serendipitous—introducing users to new and unexpected delights that seem tailor-made.

As much as these recommendation systems enhance our convenience and enjoyment, they also come with their set of challenges. One significant concern is the "filter bubble" effect, where users are continually fed content that reinforces their existing tastes. This phenomenon can limit exposure to diverse genres and ideas, stifling the kind of cultural exploration that is crucial for a vibrant and dynamic media landscape. While algorithms aim to expand our horizons, there's an inherent tension in their operation that might inadvertently narrow them.

Another consideration is the impact on creators. As recommendation algorithms steer user attention, they wield tremendous power over which songs or films gain prominence. This influence raises questions about artistic diversity and the sustainability of less mainstream works. When algorithms favor content that fits certain predefined patterns or profiles, they may inadvertently marginalize niche or experimental art forms. It's a delicate balance between popular demand and creative expression that continues to evolve.

To counteract these effects, some platforms have begun experimenting with algorithms designed to encourage exploration beyond the usual playlists or feeds. By recommending content outside of typical preferences—or spotlighting independent artists and filmmakers—these systems can foster a richer, more inclusive media ecosystem. However, achieving this balance isn't straightforward and requires ongoing refinement and transparency in how recommendations are generated.

User agency also plays a crucial role in shaping recommendation systems. While AI offers unprecedented personalization, it essentially thrives on our active participation. Platforms are exploring ways to enhance user control, enabling customization of recommendation criteria. Users can influence what they see, hear, or experience by actively rating content, curating playlists, or providing contextual feedback, thus ensuring that AI remains an ally in discovering new art forms rather than a gatekeeper.

Furthermore, the rise of AI-driven recommendations raises ethical and privacy considerations. To deliver personalized experiences, these systems rely on extensive data collection, which can include intricate details of users' preferences, behaviors, and interactions. Ensuring this data's ethical usage and protecting user privacy form critical concerns that demand robust safeguards and transparent policies from media service providers.

Despite these challenges, the possibilities presented by AI in music and movie recommendations are indeed empowering. They democratize access to the arts, allowing even the most obscure artists to find their audience through algorithmic channels. By lowering barriers and expanding reach, AI fuels an environment where creativity can thrive and where consumers can immerse themselves in the vast spectrum of human expression.

In the future, we may even see more advanced forms of AI-assisted creativity, where users can interact with algorithms to co-create music or films, tailored to their specific emotions or desires. Such advancements foreshadow a new era of personalized artistry, where human creativity and algorithmic intelligence converge to push the boundaries of what's possible in entertainment.

As we navigate this AI-driven world, maintaining a dialogue about the role of algorithms in creativity is vital. By understanding how these systems operate and their implications, we empower ourselves to engage with them critically and responsibly. The age of personalized media might seem overwhelming, but it's an opportunity to embrace technological evolution while preserving the essence of human creativity and diversity. AI in music and movie recommendations isn't just a technological marvel; it's a catalyst for a journey into uncharted realms of artistry and cultural exploration.

Chapter 13:
AI and Security

As technology advances at a breakneck pace, AI's role in security has become both a guardian and a challenge. On one hand, AI-driven cybersecurity systems are the new sentinels, tirelessly monitoring networks to detect and counteract potential threats with unprecedented speed and accuracy. These systems learn from each attempted breach, continuously evolving to anticipate and neutralize the next one. On the other hand, AI's capability for surveillance raises profound privacy concerns, as it melds with sophisticated monitoring tools that can track individual movements, habits, and interactions. This duality presents a complex landscape where the potential for enhanced protection collides with the erosion of personal privacy. Navigating this delicate balance requires us to consider not only the technological advancements but also the ethical frameworks that govern their deployment, ensuring that security does not inadvertently morph into an omnipresent, unchecked gaze. Thus, as we venture deeper into the AI-driven future, the quest for security must be harmoniously aligned with the fundamental rights and freedoms that define our humanity.

AI in Cybersecurity

The digital landscape is ever-changing, and as technology evolves, so do the threats that lurk within it. Cybersecurity has become one of the pressing concerns of our era, especially as societies and businesses increasingly rely on the interconnectedness facilitated by the internet. In this fast-paced environment, artificial intelligence offers new solutions and strategies that were previously unimaginable. AI has the ability to revolutionize the field of cybersecurity by enhancing the ability to detect, prevent, and respond to cyber threats in real time.

Traditionally, cybersecurity relied heavily on rule-based systems that were quite effective at handling known threats. However, with the advent of more sophisticated attack vectors and the proliferation of zero-day exploits, static defenses have struggled to keep pace. This is where AI steps in, providing dynamic, adaptable systems capable of learning and evolving as new threats emerge. Using machine learning algorithms, these advanced systems can analyze vast amounts of data to detect anomalies that may indicate potential breaches. This automated vigilance reduces the time required to respond to threats, which is essential in preventing data theft and damage.

One of the key advantages AI brings to cybersecurity is its capacity for pattern recognition. Cyber attackers often leave behind a trail of digital breadcrumbs, and while these can sometimes be subtle, AI excels at discerning patterns that might elude human analysts. Through techniques such as anomaly detection and behavioral analysis, AI can identify unusual network traffic or user behavior that could point to a security compromise. For example, an AI-driven system might recognize an unauthorized user mimicking the behavior of an individual employee or access attempts from unusual geographic locations.

But AI in cybersecurity isn't solely about defense; it's also a powerful tool for offense. Ethical hacking, an essential component of penetration testing, now leverages AI to simulate attacks and identify vulnerabilities within systems. By using AI tools, cybersecurity professionals can automate repetitive tasks, freeing up human expertise for strategic decision-making and allowing for more frequent and comprehensive vulnerability assessments.

Grand leaps in natural language processing (NLP) also contribute to the AI-driven cybersecurity arsenal. NLP techniques can sift through human language data, such as emails and text messages, to detect phishing attempts and other social engineering tactics. Phishing attacks have become increasingly sophisticated, often bypassing traditional spam filters. AI can improve detection rates by learning to understand the nuances of human language, recognizing suspicious phrasing or unusual requests for personal information.

Moreover, AI's deep learning capabilities are crucial in identifying malware. Traditional detection methods, which rely on signature-based systems, sometimes struggle with new and rapidly evolving malware. AI-based solutions, however, can analyze the behavior of a program rather than just its code. This behavioral analysis allows security tools to detect and isolate new malware strains that have yet to be cataloged, thereby reducing the risk of them spreading within a network.

While the promises of AI in cybersecurity are immense, they aren't without challenges and ethical considerations. One major concern is the potential for these technologies to be used maliciously. Cybercriminals are increasingly adopting AI to launch more sophisticated attacks, utilizing AI to develop highly adaptive malware or to bolster phishing schemes, making them more plausible and harder to detect. This arms race between attackers and defenders ensures that the cybersecurity battleground remains a rapidly evolving domain.

Furthermore, there's a critical need for transparency and accountability in AI-driven cybersecurity solutions. AI systems are often criticized for being blackboxes, where decision-making processes remain opaque both to those who use them and those who are affected by them. Building transparency into AI systems is crucial for gaining trust from users and ensuring that these tools are used responsibly. There's also the dilemma of false positives, where benign activities may be flagged as threats, causing unnecessary panic and possibly leading to decision fatigue among cybersecurity teams.

The successful integration of AI into cybersecurity strategies also demands a skilled workforce capable of understanding both the technology and the ethical considerations. This highlights the importance of continuous education and training in AI and cybersecurity for professionals who aim to tackle these evolving threats. Encouraging collaboration between tech companies, academia, and governments can empower the next generation of cybersecurity experts to harness AI responsibly and effectively.

Regulatory frameworks can additionally play a vital role in ensuring the ethical application of AI in cybersecurity. As AI solutions become more widespread, there should be clear guidelines that promote transparency, data privacy, and accountability, preventing misuse while encouraging innovation. Policymakers must find a balance that protects citizens and businesses without stifling technological progress.

AI in cybersecurity is not just a technological advancement; it's a vital component of our global digital infrastructure that holds profound implications for the safety and privacy of society. Its potential to adapt and learn from complex data reshapes how we envisage digital defense, offering a proactive approach that keeps pace with an ever-growing range of threats. As we continue to weave AI into the fabric of cybersecurity, the challenge will be ensuring it's used to promote a safer cyber environment for everyone.

Surveillance and Privacy Concerns

The rapid advancement of artificial intelligence has brought us to a crossroads where privacy concerns are no longer just hypothetical scenarios. Whether it's the ubiquitous presence of surveillance cameras on city streets or the invisible tracking abilities of our digital devices, AI stands at the forefront of this new reality. In today's algorithm-driven world, what was once unthinkable—constant monitoring and analysis of personal behavior—is now part of ordinary life.

AI technologies are predominantly powered by data, and vast amounts of it. This imperative for data collection has made privacy a focal point of debate and anxiety. The more information AI systems can access, the better they can perform. However, this comes at the expense of personal privacy, leading us to a crucial question: How much privacy are we willing to compromise for the conveniences and benefits AI promises?

Let's consider AI deployment in public spaces. Surveillance systems enhanced with AI can identify individuals, track their movements, and analyze their behavior in real time. Law enforcement agencies, for instance, are increasingly employing facial recognition technologies. While these systems can be invaluable for crime prevention and solving cases, the potential for misuse and overreach is significant. There are concerns about biometric data being collected without individuals' consent, thus infringing upon personal freedoms.

Furthermore, the impact extends beyond the realm of public safety. With AI's capacity to mine and analyze vast datasets, there's potential for profiling and discrimination based on race, gender, or socioeconomic status. These practices can perpetuate existing biases, leading to a loss of trust in not just the technology but the institutions that deploy them. By understanding these risks, we can better navigate the fine line between harnessing the allure of AI and safeguarding our fundamental rights.

In the digital world, AI enables targeted advertising by analyzing user behavior across websites and applications. Companies gain insights into personal preferences and shopping habits, often without explicit consent from individuals. This data collection isn't just passive; it's an active process that can influence behavior, encouraging consumers toward products they might not otherwise consider. Here, transparency becomes pivotal—users should be informed about what data is being gathered and how it is used.

However, it's not all dystopian gloom. There are voices rallying for stronger regulatory frameworks to ensure privacy isn't overshadowed by the capabilities of AI. Europe, for instance, leads the charge with its General Data Protection Regulation (GDPR), which mandates strict guidelines on data privacy. Companies must be transparent about data collection, and individuals have the right to access their data and request its deletion. Such regulations provide a blueprint for how privacy can coexist with technological progress.

Yet, legislation alone isn't enough. Public awareness and vigilance are crucial. Individuals should be empowered to safeguard their privacy actively. This means being judicious about the technologies they engage with and demanding accountability from service providers. Technology companies, on their part, must design AI systems with privacy in mind—prioritizing principles like data minimization and anonymization.

In corporate settings, the use of AI for employee monitoring is another area of profound concern. Companies employ AI to track productivity, communications, and even predict employee burnout. While these technologies can enhance efficiency and wellbeing, they risk intruding into personal space. Employees may feel monitored in ways that could impact their mental health and job satisfaction. Here, transparency and ethical guidelines should underpin AI deployment to maintain trust and workplace harmony.

While privacy advocates campaign for control over personal information, there's also a conversation to be had about the ownership of data itself. Should individuals have the right to own and control every aspect of their digital footprint, or does it inherently belong to the platforms where the data is collected? Resolving this question will define the future interactions between AI systems and the people they are meant to serve.

Educational campaigns could play a vital role in this evolving landscape. As AI technologies become more integrated into everyday life, enhancing public understanding will be pivotal. Nonprofits, educational institutions, and governments should provide resources to help individuals grasp how AI affects privacy. This deepens the dialogue between tech creators and users, promoting a more balanced power dynamic.

In sum, the challenges of surveillance and privacy concerns in the context of AI ask us to ponder the role we want these technologies to play in our society. By advocating for transparency, strong regulations, and public education, we can navigate these complexities. While AI offers unparalleled innovation and improvements to quality of life, it mustn't come at the expense of individual autonomy and freedom. Crafting an AI-centric world that respects privacy is a shared responsibility—one that calls for collaboration between policymakers, businesses, and society at large.

Chapter 14:
Social Implications of AI

As artificial intelligence continues to weave itself into the fabric of daily life, its social implications demand thoughtful examination. AI has the power to amplify existing social inequalities, potentially exacerbating the divide between those who can leverage its benefits and those left in the digital shadows. With AI systems increasingly shaping decisions across education, employment, and access to essential services, there is a risk of perpetuating biases if these systems are not designed and implemented with care. The challenge lies not only in bridging the digital divide but also in ensuring equitable access to the opportunities AI presents. As we navigate this transformative era, society must pursue proactive measures to mitigate disparities, fostering an environment where AI can be a tool for empowerment rather than division. Recognizing the potential for both harm and benefit, we are tasked with creating inclusive technologies that resonate with fairness and transparency for all. This journey demands that we remain vigilant, drawing on diverse perspectives to craft a future where AI acts as a bridge rather than a barrier.

AI and Social Inequality

As artificial intelligence continues to weave itself into the very fabric of daily life, it's crucial to address one of its most significant social implications: inequality. AI, while a powerful tool for innovation and efficiency, can also exacerbate existing social inequities if not developed and deployed thoughtfully. The technology has the potential to revolutionize industries, democratize information, and increase productivity. Yet, the same AI technologies can reflect and magnify societal biases, leading to further entrenchment of social divides.

It begins with data. AI systems learn from large datasets, and if these datasets contain biases, the AI systems will mimic them. For instance, if historical hiring data underrepresents certain groups, an AI-driven recruitment tool might perpetuate this trend, leading to unfair employment practices. Additionally, facial recognition technology, which is proliferating in both public and private sectors, has been criticized for higher error rates among non-white populations, highlighting how biased data can result in discriminatory technology.

Moreover, the deployment of AI could widen the gap between those who have access to digital tools and those who don't. As more sectors rely on AI to make critical decisions, from healthcare diagnostics to educational assessments, those who lack access to these technologies may find themselves at a significant disadvantage. This digital divide isn't just about having or not having technology—it's about the unequal ability to harness AI's benefits, exacerbating disparities in wealth, education, and opportunity.

But AI's influence on inequality doesn't stop at access and bias. The automation of jobs poses another challenge. While AI creates new jobs in fields like AI development and data science, it also threatens existing ones, particularly those that can be easily automated. Workers in roles involving routine and manual tasks are most vulnerable, often those who are already socioeconomically disadvantaged. While some argue that AI will create more jobs than it eliminates, the transition period could be tumultuous, disproportionately affecting lower-income workers and potentially driving deeper economic inequality.

It's essential to consider not just economic inequality but also disparities in power and control over AI systems. Tech companies, mostly concentrated in a few regions globally, wield immense influence over the development and deployment of AI technologies. This concentration of power raises critical questions about whose interests are prioritized in AI development. Are these technologies being built to serve the public good, or are they primarily designed to maximize profits for the few?

Legislation and policy are crucial in addressing these challenges. Regulating AI to ensure transparency, fairness, and accountability can help mitigate its potential to exacerbate inequalities. By developing frameworks that prioritize ethical AI use, policymakers can create environments where AI serves as an equalizer rather than a divider. However, crafting effective policies requires international cooperation and a nuanced understanding of AI's societal impacts.

There is also room for optimism. If harnessed correctly, AI can actually play a role in reducing social inequalities. For example, AI can improve access to high-quality education through personalized learning tools, breaking barriers for students in under-resourced areas. In healthcare, AI could democratize access to medical expertise, helping to bridge gaps in healthcare availability worldwide.

One of the keys to leveraging AI for equity lies in ensuring diverse participation in its development and deployment. By including voices from a wide range of socioeconomic and cultural backgrounds, AI systems can be designed to better reflect and serve diverse needs. Diversity in tech isn't just a matter of ethical responsibility—it's a practical necessity for building AI that supports inclusive societies.

Education must also evolve to equip individuals with the skills necessary to thrive in an AI-driven world. This includes not only technological literacy but also an understanding of AI's social, ethical, and economic implications. By preparing future generations to engage critically with AI, society can guard against potential inequities and harness AI as a force for good.

In summary, while AI holds the potential to perpetuate existing inequalities, it also offers opportunities to address them. By prioritizing fairness in AI development, ensuring equitable access, and fostering a diverse technological workforce, society can work towards an AI future that benefits everyone. Thoughtful engagement with AI's social implications is not only beneficial but necessary to build a more equitable world. The challenge lies in everyone—from individuals to governments—stepping up to meet it.

The Digital Divide

In our rapidly advancing digital age, artificial intelligence is reshaping every facet of society. Yet, amidst this progress, an ever-present challenge stands tall—the digital divide. This concept refers to the gap between individuals who have access to modern information and communication technology and those who don't. It's a gap as much about opportunity as it is about technology, and its implications are vast and multi-layered. Ignoring this divide means sidelining a significant portion of the world's population from the tools that could help them thrive in the future.

The digital divide isn't just a matter of having or lacking internet access. It encompasses a broader spectrum of issues like digital literacy, the availability of advanced devices, and the proficiency in utilizing them. While some can seamlessly integrate these technologies into their lives, others are left grappling with the unfamiliarity of AI-driven tools and platforms. This disparity can exacerbate existing social inequalities, making it an essential issue to address.

Many assume that the digital divide only affects developing countries. While it's true that infrastructure challenges in less economically developed nations amplify the divide, it would be naive to think that developed countries are immune. Urban areas often enjoy robust connectivity and tech access, but rural areas and economically disadvantaged communities within wealthy nations still struggle. The digital landscape isn't always uniform, and pockets of isolation exist everywhere.

This divide has stark implications for education. The educational landscape is shifting with AI-powered adaptive learning technologies and virtual classrooms, but without equitable access to these innovations, students in underserved areas fall further behind. The disparity doesn't just limit access to information; it narrows career opportunities and socio-economic mobility over time, baking in inequality at a systemic level.

Economic implications of the digital divide are profound, influencing both job markets and industrial innovations. Businesses increasingly rely on AI and digital platforms to drive growth. Employees proficient in tech thrive, while those lacking digital skills watch opportunities slip away. The divide influences national economies too, with digitally mature countries sprinting ahead in innovation, leaving less equipped nations trailing.

AI can, paradoxically, both bridge and widen the divide. It has potential to democratize access to education, healthcare, and financial services. Think of AI tutors in underfunded schools or mobile health diagnostics reaching remote locations. But without careful implementation and equitable access, AI might exacerbate inequalities. The same tools that uplift some could unknowingly suppress others, creating a cycle of technological disenfranchisement.

Governmental policies play a pivotal role in addressing the digital divide. Strategically planned infrastructure investments, subsidy programs for digital devices and internet access, and initiatives aimed at boosting digital literacy can narrow the gap. However, it's not just about policies on paper. Successful implementation requires multi-stakeholder collaborations, including private companies, NGOs, and community leaders.

Efforts to bridge the divide should also focus on reshaping educational curriculums. Modern education should arm students not just with traditional knowledge but also digital literacy and critical thinking skills needed in an AI-dominated world. Such skills are essential in fostering a society that can engage with technology meaningfully rather than passively consuming it.

A crucial aspect often overlooked in discussions about the digital divide is the cultural aspect. Merely providing access isn't enough. Individuals and communities need to see value in integrating technology into their lives. Cultural acceptance can be a barrier as formidable as technological infrastructure, necessitating tailored initiatives that resonate with and respect local values and practices.

Corporate social responsibility could play a transformative role here. As businesses are some of the primary beneficiaries of a digitally literate and connected population, investing in bridging this divide is not just ethical but economically strategic. Initiatives that provide affordable technology and training align long-term corporate interests with broader societal well-being.

The road to closing the digital divide is long, fraught with challenges, and requires concerted effort from multiple fronts. It's about more than cables and computers; it's about empowerment. Every new node of connectivity is a beacon of opportunity, illuminating paths for innovation, discovery, and growth. The objective isn't just to level the playing field but to create an inclusive environment where all voices contribute to shaping the digital future.

Chapter 15:
AI in Agriculture

The fields of agriculture and AI are converging in a fascinating partnership, shaping a new era where technology meets tradition. AI is revolutionizing agriculture by enabling precision farming techniques that gather and analyze data from sensors and drones to optimize crop yields while minimizing resource use. This shift isn't just about efficiency; it's a vital step toward sustainable farming practices that respond to the pressing challenges of climate change and a growing global population. Imagine farms where AI predicts weather patterns, detects plant diseases early, and tailors irrigation precisely, all contributing to healthier crops with reduced ecological footprints. Farmers, often seen as guardians of nature, are becoming data-driven innovators, utilizing artificial intelligence to ensure food security while stewarding the land for future generations. Through AI, agriculture not only feeds the present but also seeds a sustainable future.

Precision Agriculture Techniques

As the sun rises over vast expanses of farmland, a quiet revolution is underway. Precision agriculture, a term that's rapidly gaining traction, represents a significant shift in how farming is done. At its core, precision agriculture is about using advanced technology, including AI and machine learning, to optimize the efficiency and productivity of farming practices. It's a nuanced approach that tailors experimentation and decision-making to the needs of individual plots, rather than treating an entire field uniformly.

Imagine drones buzzing over fields, capturing imagery to analyze crop health in real-time. These drones are equipped with hyperspectral cameras and sensors, each capturing specific data points. With this technology, farmers are empowered to identify the exact spots suffering from pests, diseases, or nutrient deficiency. By targeting these problem areas with precision, inputs like fertilizers and pesticides are used more efficiently, reducing waste and environmental impact.

But drones are only part of the story. Soil sensors, adept at monitoring moisture levels and soil composition, also play a critical role in precision agriculture. Placed strategically throughout a field, these sensors provide real-time data, helping farmers decide when and where to irrigate. Not only does this conserve water—a resource that's becoming increasingly scarce—but it also ensures crops are nourished without oversaturation.

The use of AI models in precision agriculture is transforming how data is interpreted and applied. Machine learning algorithms analyze the data collected by drones and sensors to predict yields, detect disease outbreaks, and recommend the best planting and harvesting times. These algorithms learn from historical data, calibrating their predictions based on past results and seasonal variations, allowing for a dynamic response to changing conditions.

Satellite imagery, another technological marvel enhancing precision agriculture, provides a macro perspective. These images, collected regularly, allow farmers to monitor crop growth stages, assess biomass, and evaluate overall field productivity. At their disposal is a rich tapestry of information, layered and analyzed to guide strategic decisions. While seemingly straightforward, the integration of satellite data with ground-level sensors produces a powerful decision-making tool for agriculturalists.

Artificial intelligence doesn't stop at data analysis; it extends to predictive analytics and automated systems. For instance, AI-driven robotic systems can handle tasks such as planting and weeding autonomously. These robots perform with a degree of precision and consistency unattainable by manual labor. Autonomous tractors, also powered by AI, can plow fields with pinpoint accuracy, following pre-determined patterns that optimize land use and minimize fuel consumption.

Precision agriculture also leans heavily on big data analytics. Vast datasets, including weather patterns, historical yield statistics, and market trends, provide farmers with insights into every facet of their operations. This analytical power allows them not only to react to current conditions but to forecast future challenges and opportunities. In an industry often dictated by uncontrollable variables, predictive analytics offers a semblance of control, allowing farmers to hedge against risks and optimize profits.

However, the journey to implement precision agriculture isn't free from challenges. High initial costs and the integration of sophisticated technologies pose barriers, especially for small-scale farmers. There's a learning curve as well; mastering new technology doesn't happen overnight. Farmers must adapt and acquire new skills, which sometimes involves overcoming skepticism about whether these technologies will bring promised improvements.

Interoperability issues also arise with disparate systems and technologies within precision agriculture. Ensuring these different technologies communicate effectively is vital for a seamless operational process. As standardization within this field is still evolving, technology providers and farmers alike are navigating through these complexities, working towards more cohesive and integrated solutions.

There's also the question of data privacy and ownership. As precision agriculture increasingly relies on large volumes of data, concerns regarding who owns and controls this data become paramount. Ensuring farmers retain access and control over their farm's data is crucial, protecting them from potential exploitation by large tech firms.

Despite these hurdles, the potential benefits of precision agriculture are too significant to ignore. Reduced environmental impact, optimized resource use, and enhanced productivity can transform the agricultural sector. Furthermore, incorporating AI in agriculture is key to addressing global challenges such as food security in an era of climate change and growing populations.

The narrative of precision agriculture is still unfolding, evolving as technology progresses. What began as a novel concept is gradually permeating the agricultural industry, driven by necessity and innovation. As artificial intelligence continues to evolve, so too will its applications in precision agriculture, ushering in a future where farming is as much about bytes and algorithms as it is about seeds and soil.

AI and Sustainable Farming

Artificial intelligence has emerged as a transformative force in agriculture, helping farmers tackle longstanding challenges while paving the way for sustainable farming practices. As the global population continues to grow, there's an ever-increasing demand for food, which in turn pressures agricultural ecosystems. Traditional farming methods, while effective to a point, often strain resources and contribute to issues like soil degradation, water scarcity, and pollution. AI offers innovative solutions, enabling farmers to enhance productivity and sustainability while minimizing environmental impact.

One of the most significant ways AI contributes to sustainable farming is through precision agriculture. By integrating advanced data analytics and machine learning, AI systems provide farmers with accurate insights into crop health, soil quality, and weather patterns. This data-driven approach allows for more precise application of water, fertilizer, and pesticides, reducing waste and mitigating harmful environmental effects. With AI's help, farmers can make informed decisions that optimize resource use and increase crop yields, leading to both economic and ecological benefits.

Moreover, AI technologies enable the development of autonomous farming equipment that can perform tasks such as planting, watering, and harvesting with unmatched precision. These machines use sensors and GPS technology to navigate fields efficiently, reducing fuel usage and limiting soil compaction—a critical factor in maintaining healthy soil structure. Additionally, drones equipped with AI capabilities can monitor large farm areas, collect real-time data, and provide invaluable insights into crop conditions. These AI-powered tools streamline farm operations and drastically reduce labor costs, making sustainable farming practices more accessible and economically feasible.

Water conservation is another area where AI plays a crucial role in sustainable agriculture. As water scarcity becomes an increasing concern, AI-powered irrigation systems help farmers use water more judiciously. By analyzing weather forecasts, soil moisture levels, and plant water requirements, these intelligent systems can determine the optimal irrigation schedule. This precision in water management not only conserves water resources but also ensures that crops receive adequate hydration, leading to healthier plant growth and improved resilience against drought conditions.

In addition to improving resource efficiency, AI-driven solutions also support biodiversity in agricultural systems. By adopting AI-based monitoring technologies, farmers can create more diverse and resilient ecosystems. These systems track the presence of different plant and animal species, identifying potential threats and imbalances within the ecosystem. With this insight, farmers can implement integrated pest management practices, reducing reliance on chemical pesticides and promoting natural predator-prey relationships. Protecting biodiversity ensures long-term agricultural productivity and enhances the resilience of farming systems in the face of environmental changes.

Yet, integrating AI into sustainable farming is not without its challenges. Farmers must overcome barriers such as the cost of technology adoption, data privacy concerns, and the need for training and education in AI technologies. Collaborative efforts between tech companies, governments, and research institutions are essential to address these challenges and make AI tools accessible to farmers at all levels. By investing in AI education and infrastructure, stakeholders can empower farmers to leverage these technologies effectively, further promoting sustainable agriculture practices.

There's also an ethical dimension to consider as AI becomes more embedded in agricultural practices. As with any AI application, algorithmic transparency and accountability must be prioritized to ensure fairness and trust. Stakeholders must remain vigilant to prevent data monopolization and protect farmers' rights to access and control their information. Ensuring ethical use of AI is crucial to fostering an equitable agricultural revolution that benefits everyone involved, from smallholder farmers to large agricultural enterprises.

Looking toward the future, AI holds promise for even more groundbreaking advancements in sustainable agriculture. One such frontier is the development of AI-based predictive models that can simulate various farming scenarios, guiding farmers in planning and crop selection. These models could provide insights into which crops are best suited for specific environmental conditions, aiding in the adaptation to climate change. Furthermore, continuous advancements in AI could lead to the creation of self-learning systems that autonomously adjust farming strategies in real-time, maximizing both yield and soil health.

AI's footprint in sustainable agriculture not only enhances productivity but also supports the creation of resilient and adaptable agricultural systems. As this technology continues to evolve, it offers novel ways to tackle the complex interconnections between agriculture and the environment. Through collaborative and inclusive approaches, AI can drive a shift towards more regenerative farming practices that honor the planet's ecological boundaries, ensuring food security for future generations.

In conclusion, AI represents a powerful ally in the quest for sustainable farming, offering tools that improve efficiency and reduce environmental impact. By integrating these technologies into agriculture, we not only meet the current food demands but also lay the groundwork for a more sustainable future. Embracing AI's potential in agriculture requires cooperation, ethical oversight, and a willingness to innovate. With these efforts, AI can lead us toward resilient agricultural practices that nourish both people and the planet.

Chapter 16:
AI in Finance

In the vast world of finance, artificial intelligence is reshaping how we understand and interact with money. From analyzing soaring volumes of stock market data to automating mundane banking processes, AI is crafting a new era of financial intelligence and efficiency. The algorithms sift through complex datasets with unparalleled speed, revealing market trends and investment opportunities that were once obscured by their sheer volume and intricacy. As a result, the precision with which financial forecasts are made has increased, allowing investors and institutions to make informed decisions swiftly and accurately. In banking, AI-driven automation reduces human error, improves customer service through chatbots, and enhances security by detecting fraudulent activities with acute precision. This technological transformation isn't just about improving bottom lines; it's about redefining trust and accessibility in the financial sector, aiming to create a more inclusive economic environment. Through AI, finance is not simply evolving; it is being reimagined, ushering us into an era where the traditional boundaries of financial ecosystems fade, making way for innovation and possibility.

AI in Stock Market Analysis

In the high-stakes world of stock market trading, the infusion of artificial intelligence has profoundly transformed the landscape. Traditionally, investors and traders relied heavily on fundamental and technical analysis, which required sifting through financial statements, scrutinizing historical price patterns, and even relying on gut feelings. Today, AI provides new dimensions of analysis, offering unprecedented insights and predictive capabilities that are reshaping strategies.

At the core of this transformation is machine learning, a subset of AI that enables systems to learn from data. By processing vast amounts of historical market data, AI models can detect patterns impossible for humans to discern. These models, capable of learning and adapting, allow investors to predict market trends more accurately and respond swiftly, ensuring minimal losses and maximized gains.

Yet, the formidable strength of AI lies not just in processing and prediction but also in its ability to handle minute details at a colossal scale. High-frequency trading, for instance, benefits immensely from AI technologies. It involves executing trades in fractions of a second, a pace unmatchable by human traders. Here, AI algorithms leverage big data and rapid-speed analysis to make split-second decisions, banking on tiny price changes to turn significant profits.

Moreover, the advent of natural language processing (NLP) allows AI to make sense of textual data, like news articles, social media chatter, and market reports, integrating them into trading strategies. An unexpected tweet or news flash can send stocks plummeting or soaring. AI systems equipped with NLP capabilities can digest and interpret this flood of information in real time, providing traders with sentiment analysis and calibrated market responses.

Despite AI's analytical prowess, the stock market remains a complex beast. Factors influencing stock prices are not only numerous but are often bound by human sentiment and unpredictable geopolitical events. AI models face significant challenges in anticipating black swan events—unpredictable occurrences that have major ramifications. Thus, while AI can augment decision-making, it doesn't fully eliminate the risks involved in trading.

Ethics also come into play, particularly concerning algorithmic trading. AI's capacity to execute trades rapidly and autonomously raises questions about fairness and market stability. For instance, how does one keep a market fair when algorithms are designed to consistently outpace human competition? There's an ongoing debate on regulating AI in trading to prevent scenarios like the infamous "Flash Crash" of 2010, where algorithmic trading led to a sharp market dip within minutes.

In addition to ethical considerations, transparency in AI models is crucial. Often, AI operates as a black box, with little insight into its decision-making process. For investors, understanding the rationale behind a trading decision is essential. Thus, developing explainable AI (XAI) systems that offer clarity on AI-generated trading signals is essential for building trust and reliability in the technology.

Some of the most successful firms in the financial sector are now those that effectively integrate AI into their trading platforms. Noteworthy companies have crafted proprietary algorithms that create a robust competitive edge. These AI systems can scan multiple financial markets simultaneously, maintaining a watchful eye for arbitrage opportunities that others might miss. It's a game of milliseconds, where the savvy use of technology is imperative to stay ahead.

However, AI in stock market analysis isn't just for the giants. Retail investors also benefit from AI-driven tools. There are platforms providing AI-powered financial advice, portfolio management solutions, and even robo-advisors that democratize access to sophisticated trading algorithms once exclusive to institutional investors. This accessibility allows the average person to partake in market opportunities traditionally reserved for seasoned traders.

As we move forward, the collaboration between humans and machines in market analysis is the key. While AI can process data at lightning speeds, human oversight ensures that strategic decisions account for experience, ethical considerations, and foresight. This partnership embodies the ideal of human-AI collaboration, where each complements the other's strengths.

Thus, as AI continues to evolve, so too will its role in the stock market. By leveraging AI's capabilities, investors and traders can not only optimize their portfolios but can also push the boundaries of what traditional analysis could achieve. The potential for innovation in this domain is boundless, offering exciting prospects for the future of finance.

Automation in Banking

At the heart of modern finance, the banking industry has embraced automation with vigor and optimism, transforming an age-old institution into a beacon of technological advancement. Automation, driven by artificial intelligence (AI), is fundamentally reshaping how banks operate, interact with customers, and safeguard information. From humble beginnings, merely routing calls or managing minor transactions, automation now permeates almost every aspect of banking. But what does this mean for the average consumer and the industry as a whole?

One of the most noticeable shifts is the enhanced customer experience. Gone are the days when banking required a physical presence at a branch; today, most transactions can be completed from the comfort of one's home or even on the go. AI-powered chatbots, available 24/7, have revolutionized customer service by handling inquiries, resolving issues, and providing personalized financial advice. These digital assistants learn from each interaction, becoming increasingly adept at responding to complex queries with speed and precision.

Beyond customer interaction, automation is optimizing operational efficiency in back offices. AI algorithms are masterfully streamlining processes such as loan approvals, risk management, and fraud detection. By analyzing massive datasets rapidly and accurately, AI can provide insights that were once elusive to even the most seasoned financial analysts. This not only reduces costs but also leads to more robust and secure banking systems. The predictive capabilities of AI help banks proactively address potential risks, safeguarding assets and enhancing regulatory compliance.

Despite the clear benefits, the rise of automation in banking raises questions and concerns. There are worries about data privacy, given the sensitive nature of financial information. As banks rely more heavily on algorithms, ensuring the protection of this data from breaches becomes paramount. Additionally, the transition to an automated workforce impacts employment within the sector. Many traditional roles are at risk, replaced by AI-driven systems. However, this shift also creates opportunities. Banks are investing in retraining their workforce to work alongside AI, emphasizing the strategic, high-touch, human-centered aspects of banking that machines can't replicate.

Financial inclusion is another intriguing aspect of automation in banking. AI has the potential to bring banking services to unbanked or underbanked populations across the globe. With smartphone penetration and mobile banking platforms, individuals in remote or underserved areas can access financial services once beyond their reach. This development promises a more equitable financial landscape, where everyone has potential access to mainstream banking and its benefits.

However, the path to full automation and financial inclusion is not without obstacles. Technological infrastructure, particularly in developing regions, needs to be bolstered. Considerations around digital literacy must also be addressed to allow individuals to effectively navigate automated systems. The role of policymakers and regulatory bodies is crucial here, as they shape frameworks that balance innovation with consumer protection.

Partnerships between banks and fintech companies are burgeoning, reshaping the competitive landscape. Traditional banks are collaborating with tech-savvy startups, combining their trust-based legacy with cutting-edge technology to offer innovative solutions. These collaborations are accelerating the pace at which automation trends are implemented, creating a dynamic environment ripe with possibility.

Looking ahead, the future of banking lies in 'smart contracts' and blockchain technologies. These innovations promise even greater transparency and efficiency. Smart contracts, powered by blockchain, can automatically execute transactions and enforce the terms of agreements without human intervention. This could significantly reduce costs and errors, while also enhancing the security and trust of financial transactions.

The benefits of automation in banking are vast and varied, but it's not simply about machines taking over tasks. Instead, it's about creating a symbiotic relationship between humans and technology, where AI enhances human capabilities, offering unprecedented levels of service, security, and convenience. By embracing these changes thoughtfully and responsibly, the banking industry stands to revolutionize how we think about money, savings, and investments in a profoundly transformative way.

In conclusion, automation in banking holds the promise of a more efficient, inclusive, and secure financial future, if navigated wisely. It's imperative for stakeholders—banks, consumers, and regulators—to actively engage in dialogues that shape the trajectory of these advancements. The potential benefits are immense, charting a new course that could democratize financial services on a scale never seen before. The journey toward an AI-driven banking landscape is just beginning, and it's set to redefine industry norms, consumer expectations, and economic landscapes for generations to come.

Chapter 17:
Global Perspectives on AI

The landscape of artificial intelligence is as diverse as the nations harnessing its potential, each tailoring AI development to fit its unique cultural, economic, and political contexts. From China's ambitious AI ambitions aiming to dominate global markets, to Europe's stringent data protection frameworks such as GDPR, national AI strategies reveal both the innovative promise and the pragmatic challenges nations face. While some countries compete fiercely to lead in technological advances, others collaborate through international partnerships to ensure ethical AI usage and equitable access. This global mosaic of AI reflects a dynamic interplay of cooperation and rivalry, prompting rich discussions on how societies can collectively navigate the intricate web of AI governance. As we witness these developments, it's clear that understanding AI from a global perspective provides invaluable insights into shaping a future where technology aligns with humanity's shared values and aspirations.

AI Policies Around the World

In a world that is rapidly becoming more interconnected, diverse approaches to artificial intelligence (AI) governance highlight not just policy differences but also cultural, economic, and social variations. Each country's approach reflects its unique priorities, resources, and even historical narrative. These distinct paths paint a global mosaic of

AI development that transcends mere technology implementation and delves into the ethics and challenges that each nation prioritizes.

At the forefront of AI policy leadership is the European Union (EU), which has made significant efforts to craft comprehensive legislation regarding AI. The EU's approach is distinctly characterized by a focus on ethical AI usage and the protection of individual privacy rights. The General Data Protection Regulation (GDPR), though not specific to AI, forms a foundation for how personal data associated with AI systems should be managed. Moreover, the EU's proposed AI regulatory framework seeks to classify AI systems based on risk levels—from systems that pose minimal risk to those that could significantly impact individual rights or safety. This tiered approach ensures that AI systems are subject to scrutiny proportional to their potential for harm, setting a precedent for other regions.

Meanwhile, in the United States, AI policy is predominantly shaped by innovation incentives rather than strict regulation. The U.S. operates under a more decentralized governance model where federal guidelines provide a broad framework, while specific implementations and applications are driven by state legislation and industry initiatives. This approach nurtures an environment of rapid technological advancement, fostering significant AI-driven economic contributions. However, this same approach can sometimes lead to inconsistencies in privacy protection and ethical standards across different sectors.

China presents another unique model, intertwining AI policy with national interest goals. The Chinese government's strategy is underpinned by a goal to become the world leader in AI development and application by 2030. This ambition translates into substantial government investments in AI research and industry. Additionally, China's AI strategy uniquely emphasizes social stability and national security, resulting in applications that heavily integrate into surveillance and social governance frameworks. While this fosters technological prowess, it also raises significant international concern regarding individual freedoms and privacy.

Globally, approaches in developing countries offer a different perspective, where AI policy is frequently framed within a context of economic development and capacity building. Nations in Africa and South America, for instance, are increasingly focusing on leveraging AI for key sectors like agriculture, healthcare, and public infrastructure. Partnerships with international and non-governmental organizations become critical to support these ambitions, given limited local resources and expertise. Here, AI is viewed as a bridge to overcome infrastructural and logistical challenges, potentially leapfrogging traditional development hurdles.

Japan and South Korea represent nations that blend technology innovation with societal needs, focusing heavily on AI applications for aging populations and enhancing quality of life. Policies in these countries prioritize the integration of AI in care provision, aiming to address demographic changes that challenge traditional workforce structures and resource allocations. The cultural acceptance of robots and AI in everyday life further supports these policy priorities, fostering an environment where technology is seen as a complement rather than a replacement for human effort.

India, as an emerging AI player, balances its policies with a focus on inclusivity and societal impact. The Indian government's AI strategy emphasizes using AI to serve the underprivileged and improve access to essential services like education and healthcare. This vision is supported by initiatives to expand AI literacy and minimize potential disruptions in an economy that still heavily relies on human labor. India's approach highlights the importance of ensuring technological progression does not amplify socio-economic divides.

The diversity in AI policy approaches isn't merely a consequence of differing economic capabilities or governance models; it embodies varied national identities and cultural values. For instance, countries with strong democratic traditions often prioritize individual rights, pushing ethical AI considerations to the fore. On the other hand, nations focusing on economic pragmatism may pursue AI deployment with fewer immediate concerns about ethical ramifications, instead prioritizing cyber sovereignty and economic competitiveness.

International cooperation in AI policy is another critical domain, as emerging technologies inherently cross geographical and jurisdictional boundaries. Initiatives by intergovernmental organizations, such as UNESCO's recommendations on AI ethics, aim to harmonize national policies and encourage collaboration. These efforts reflect an understanding that global challenges, including cyber threats and ethical AI deployment, require cooperative frameworks beyond national borders.

As AI continues to evolve, countries must balance innovation with regulation, ensuring that policies foster both technological advances and ethical imperatives. The ongoing dialogue about AI standards and governance is a dynamic spectrum, with each nation contributing to the broader picture based on its unique context and aspirations. Ultimately, the goal is to craft AI policies that not only protect but empower, ensuring technology serves humanity without compromising fundamental values.

International Cooperation and Competition

In an increasingly interconnected world, the race for artificial intelligence (AI) supremacy mirrors the classic dichotomy between collaboration and competition. Nations find themselves at a crossroads, poised between building alliances that advance technological capabilities globally and pursuing nationalistic agendas that prioritize their own progress. This dynamic is more than just a geopolitical chess game; it is a critical narrative that will shape the ethical, economic, and societal contours of our world.

Countries like China and the United States have emerged as leaders in AI development, each leveraging their unique strengths. China's vast pool of data, robust government funding, and ambitious national plans have propelled it to the forefront. Meanwhile, the U.S. relies on its deep-rooted innovation ecosystem, characterized by top-tier universities and a thriving startup culture. This rivalry, however, extends beyond mere technological prowess—it's about setting standards and norms that could govern AI usage globally.

Despite the apparent competition, there's growing recognition of the need for international cooperation. AI, by its very nature, transcends borders. Efforts such as the Global Partnership on Artificial Intelligence (GPAI) illustrate attempts to bring countries together to ensure AI's positive impact. These alliances seek to craft frameworks for shared ethical guidelines and best practices that can mitigate risks associated with AI technologies. International norms in AI emphasize transparency, accountability, and inclusiveness, aiming to harmonize disparate national regulations.

Yet, collaboration isn't devoid of challenges. Diverse political systems and varying degrees of technological maturity across countries can complicate consensus-building. For instance, democratic nations often face hurdles in balancing AI innovation with privacy concerns, while authoritarian regimes may prioritize control over ethical considerations. These differences further complicate the landscape of international AI policy-making, posing a question of whether it's possible to find common ground. Thus, the dialogue around AI is not just technical but deeply political.

Nevertheless, the potential benefits of international cooperation are significant. Harmonizing AI standards could facilitate trade and foster innovation, while reducing the risk of a technological cold war.

Additionally, collaborative efforts in AI research can accelerate progress in solving global challenges, such as climate change or pandemics. By pooling resources, countries can enhance their collective resilience against cyber threats or data breaches, reinforcing the global security apparatus.

Competition, on the other hand, can drive technological advancement by inspiring nations to innovate rapidly. This push for dominance often results in significant investment in research and development, leading to breakthroughs that might have otherwise taken years to achieve. The competitive edge can also stimulate public and private sector collaboration within countries, aligning resources towards national AI strategies.

Still, unbridled competition isn't without its pitfalls. A focus on gaining supremacy might lead nations to overlook ethical considerations or cut corners in safety features. There's also the threat of widening the technological gap between developed and developing countries, exacerbating global inequality. Smaller nations might struggle to keep pace, potentially leaving a majority of the world vulnerable to AI-driven power imbalances.

Given these complexities, a dual approach seems essential—a delicate balance between cooperation and competition could foster a healthy AI ecosystem globally. Strategic diplomacy and treaties will be fundamental in creating an environment where countries can achieve both national interests and shared global goals. Compromise and mutual respect will be key in ensuring that standards are inclusive and reflective of diverse perspectives.

Looking ahead, the future of international cooperation and competition in AI will heavily influence the trajectory of global development. Nations must craft policies that are not only economically advantageous but ethically sound and socially inclusive. As AI continues to evolve, so too must the frameworks governing it, ensuring they are adaptable and forward-thinking. With the right blend of strategic vision and cooperative spirit, the potential for AI to benefit humanity is boundless.

Chapter 18:
The Role of Big Data

In today's digital landscape, big data is not just a buzzword but a pivotal force that drives the efficacy and innovation of artificial intelligence. At its core, big data refers to the colossal amounts of structured and unstructured information generated every second, which when harnessed, can reveal patterns, trends, and associations, particularly relating to human behavior and interactions. AI systems thrive on such data, using it as the lifeblood to learn, adapt, and improve. However, this reliance on vast datasets also brings about crucial challenges, particularly around data privacy and security. As we navigate this data-rich era, it's imperative to strike a delicate balance between reaping the benefits of big data and safeguarding individual privacy. The conversation around big data is not just about how it fuels AI, but also about our role in shaping policies that preserve trust and ethical standards in our increasingly data-driven world. Understanding the dynamics of big data becomes not only a technological necessity but a societal imperative as well.

How Data Fuels AI

In the sprawling ecosystem of artificial intelligence (AI), data stands as the vital energy source that drives these complex systems. AI's rapid progression wouldn't be possible without the vast amounts of data that feed its algorithms. Data provides the raw inputs needed for AI models to learn, adapt, and evolve, turning abstract concepts into practical, everyday applications. It's no exaggeration to say that in AI development, data is more valuable than gold.

Understanding how data fuels AI begins with recognizing how data is collected and processed. From social media interactions to digital transactions and sensor readings, our world generates a staggering amount of data every day. This data is collected, cleaned, and curated meticulously before it becomes useful for AI systems. These preliminary steps ensure that AI models receive high-quality data, which ultimately leads to better predictions and decisions.

The sheer volume of data available today isn't the only factor fueling AI's growth—variety and velocity play just as significant a role. Traditional databases once stored data in structured formats: rows and columns that a machine could easily understand. But now, AI thrives on unstructured data—photos, videos, audio, and natural language texts—vastly expanding the types of inputs it can learn from.

Machine learning, a subset of AI, thrives on this copious data, continuously refining itself as it processes more and more inputs. The phrase "garbage in, garbage out" has never been more pertinent than in AI systems; the quality of the output heavily depends on the quality and quantity of input data. Data forms the backbone that supports the learning process where algorithms use statistical methods to uncover patterns and make predictions.

For instance, in natural language processing—AI's ability to understand and generate human language—the model's potency is reflective of the data it's trained on. By analyzing massive volumes of text, these systems gradually comprehend nuance, context, and intention, becoming more sophisticated over time. The ability to parse the complex tapestry of human language has revolutionized industries, from customer service bots to real-time language translation applications.

Moreover, image recognition, another cornerstone of AI capabilities, relies heavily on data. The identification and classification processes, whether used in medical diagnostics or autonomous vehicles, are trained on thousands, often millions, of labeled images. These datasets enable AI to achieve astonishing accuracy in identifying, say, a malignant tumor in a medical image, or a pedestrian crossing a street, minimizing errors and enhancing safety.

Importantly, data isn't static—it evolves as new information becomes available. This dynamism allows AI systems to remain flexible to changing conditions. They are not only trained using historical data but are continuously fine-tuned with new data, adapting to new problems, trends, and needs. This adaptability is perhaps one of AI's greatest attributes, allowing it to stay relevant in a rapidly changing environment.

However, the ability to harness big data for AI's advantage also brings ethical considerations to the forefront, which we'll explore further in the next sections of this book. Data privacy, ownership, and security become pressing issues as companies and governments leverage data to gain insights and guide decisions. The more AI learns from our data, the more it beckons questions about how our data is used and protected.

Despite these challenges, it's undisputed that data fundamentally transforms AI from theoretical constructs into practical, impactful solutions. It enables AI to tackle some of the world's most pressing issues, including healthcare, environmental sustainability, and personalized education. The interplay between data and AI fosters an environment ripe with potential, one where innovative solutions continually emerge.

As AI technologies advance, understanding the role of data in this landscape becomes key to understanding AI itself. It's crucial for anyone keen on mastering this digital age to grasp not just the mechanics of AI algorithms, but also the significance of the data that powers them. Our journey through AI's relationship with data continues, unveiling layers of complexity and opportunity that shape our technology-driven world.

Data Privacy Challenges

As we delve into the world of big data, the question of data privacy looms large. Big data, by its very nature, involves the collection, analysis, and storage of vast amounts of information, much of which is personal or sensitive. This unprecedented capability to gather and process data has opened up numerous possibilities for advancement in areas ranging from healthcare to marketing. However, it has also created a new frontier of challenges when it comes to protecting individual privacy.

Individual data, collected, stored, and analyzed by corporations, often without explicit or informed consent, has morphed into one of the most valuable commodities of our digital age. The challenge lies not only in securing this information from unauthorized access but also in how data is ethically used. Companies frequently find themselves balancing on a tightrope between harnessing the power of data for innovation and respecting the privacy rights of individuals.

With the exponential growth in data collection, one of the primary challenges is the sheer volume of data that needs to be managed. Companies hold extensive databases filled with detailed personal information—purchase histories, health records, and even real-time location data. Ensuring the security of these databases is paramount yet complex. A single security oversight can lead to devastating breaches, compromising thousands or even millions of records.

Furthermore, the increasingly sophisticated methods of data analysis present another layer of complexity. Through techniques like machine learning and predictive analytics, organizations can infer behavioral patterns and sensitive insights without direct input from individuals. This raises ethical questions about the extent to which such inferences should be permissible and how individuals can maintain control over their personal data.

The regulatory landscape is evolving as governments and international bodies attempt to address these privacy concerns. Legislation such as the European Union's General Data Protection Regulation (GDPR) and the California Consumer Privacy Act (CCPA) are steps towards more stringent data protection measures. These laws provide individuals with more rights over their data, such as the right to access, the right to erasure, and the right to portability. However, the global nature of data flow means that compliance with a patchwork of regulations poses its own challenges for multinational companies.

The concept of informed consent is also being scrutinized. In the digital realm, consent agreements are often buried in lengthy terms of service documents that few people read. This has led to calls for more transparent data practices that go beyond mere compliance. A genuine respect for privacy involves designing systems and processes that automatically safeguard user data while ensuring users truly understand the implications of their consent.

Innovative solutions are emerging to address these challenges. Privacy-preserving technologies such as homomorphic encryption and differential privacy are being developed to allow computations on encrypted data without revealing any of the underlying data. These technologies promise to revolutionize how companies can use data meaningfully without compromising privacy.

The challenge also extends to ensuring accountability and transparency in data handling practices. Data governance frameworks are crucial for defining how data is collected, used, shared, and kept secure. Companies must establish and rigorously enforce policies that ensure compliance with privacy laws and ethical standards, while also fostering an organizational culture that prioritizes data protection.

The increasing integration of artificial intelligence in data processing adds another dimension to privacy challenges. AI systems require vast amounts of data for training and operation, often leading to questions about the anonymization of datasets. The risk of re-identification persists even with anonymized data pools, prompting further debate on how best to protect individual identity in AI applications.

Finally, fostering public trust in data practices is crucial. The frequent news of data breaches and misuse has led to a growing skepticism among consumers. Transparent communication about how data is used and protected can help rebuild trust. Companies must demonstrate a commitment to ethical data use, aligning their strategies with public expectations for responsible data stewardship.

In conclusion, data privacy challenges are multifaceted and evolving alongside technological advancement. As we continue to rely on big data to inform decisions and drive progress, addressing these privacy challenges will require collaboration across industries, policymakers, and society. By prioritizing privacy and ethical data use, we can harness the benefits of big data while safeguarding individual rights and freedoms.

Chapter 19:
Machine Learning Basics

Diving into the world of machine learning unveils a realm where computers transcend their traditional roles, learning from data to make decisions or predictions without explicit programming. At its core, machine learning is about crafting algorithms that iteratively enhance themselves through exposure to vast datasets, akin to how humans harness experience to hone skills. This dynamic process is revolutionizing countless fields, from personalized recommendations on your favorite streaming platform to breakthrough advancements in disease diagnosis. Understanding the basic principles of machine learning empowers us to appreciate how these underlying systems detect patterns, adapt to new information, and transform ineffable insights into tangible innovations. In a world becoming ever-more reliant on data-driven approaches, grasping these fundamentals equips us to critically engage with technologies molding the fabric of our everyday lives. As we proceed, remember: at every click, every swipe, every decision aided by a smart device, machine learning quietly powers the engines of our modern existence.

Understanding Machine Learning

To truly grasp the concept of machine learning, it's essential to see past the buzzwords and delve into the mechanics that drive this fascinating branch of artificial intelligence. At its core, machine learning enables systems to learn from data, identify patterns, and make decisions with minimal human intervention. This capability stems from models that algorithms build by analyzing vast amounts of data, allowing these systems to improve their performance autonomously over time.

Understanding the building blocks of machine learning involves recognizing the types of learning methods: supervised learning, unsupervised learning, and reinforcement learning. Each type is designed to handle different tasks. Supervised learning uses labeled data to make predictions or classify information. Unsupervised learning, on the other hand, manages data without predefined labels, seeking hidden structures and relationships. Reinforcement learning operates on a system of rewards and punishments, much like a game, enabling machines to make a series of decisions that maximize a reward signal over time.

Consider supervised learning as analogous to a student working through a math problem set with the answers provided. The student, or algorithm, adjusts their approach based on which answers were correct. In contrast, unsupervised learning is akin to exploring a new topic without a guide, pulling insights together without predetermined correct answers. Reinforcement learning, however, is like playing a chess game where adjustments continue until mastering the chess strategy, as the machine refines its tactics through repeated play and feedback.

These methods, while unique in their application, all hinge upon the iterative nature of learning from data. Unlike traditional programming, where explicit instructions dictate the program's function, machine learning focuses on creating models that sift through data. These models detect patterns and derive their own rules, leading to predictions or decisions based on new inputs. This self-sufficient learning process is what distinguishes machine learning from explicit coding where every conceivable scenario requires hard coding.

The role of algorithms in machine learning is central; they are the engines driving the learning process. Algorithms iterate over data, adjust parameters, and refine their outputs through feedback. Some of the well-known algorithms include decision trees, support vector machines, and neural networks. Each of these has its strengths and ideal use cases. Decision trees are simple and effective for certain tasks, support vector machines excel in classification, and neural networks, with their layered architecture, have become synonymous with deep learning breakthroughs.

Machine learning broadly impacts various sectors, continually reshaping industries and influencing everyday life. In finance, for example, it facilitates fraud detection by identifying unusual patterns. In healthcare, it assists in diagnostics, providing insights from large datasets that might be missed by human practitioners. Retail uses it for personalized recommendations, enhancing customer experiences. Such applications extend to numerous domains, showcasing the versatility and transformative potential of machine learning.

One must acknowledge, however, the challenges accompanying the rise of machine learning. Data quality is paramount; poor data leads to inadequate models and erroneous conclusions. This dependency on high-quality, well-structured data can limit the reliability of machine learning applications. Additionally, as models become more complex, interpreting their decisions turns into a "black box" problem, where understanding the model's logic or basis for decision-making becomes opaque, posing ethical and practical issues.

The democratization of machine learning, propelled by open-source frameworks and cloud-based services, simplifies barriers to entry. Tools like TensorFlow and PyTorch allow increasingly diverse groups of people to develop and test machine learning algorithms. This accessibility furthers innovation and democratizes AI development, allowing small startups the same opportunities to experiment and iterate on machine learning models as tech giants.

As machine learning continues to evolve, it's reshaping our world in profound ways, many of which remain invisible to the casual observer. Understanding machine learning not only demystifies its processes but also empowers individuals to critically engage with the algorithm-driven world. From enhancing efficiencies in manufacturing to predicting societal trends, machine learning stands as a vital tool in embracing the future.

Applications of Machine Learning

Machine learning, a subset of artificial intelligence, has found its way into nearly every corner of our modern world. Its ability to learn patterns from data and make predictions or decisions has made it a transformative technology across countless industries. From predicting stock prices to personalizing your music playlists, machine learning is a silent architect shaping our current digital landscape.

In healthcare, machine learning applications are saving lives and improving patient outcomes. Predictive algorithms analyze vast amounts of historical data to identify disease patterns, providing doctors with crucial insights that can lead to early interventions. For instance, algorithms are used to predict the likelihood of diseases such as diabetes or cancer, often before traditional diagnostic methods can detect them. These technological advancements not only aid in diagnostics but also in personalizing treatment plans, ensuring patients receive the most effective care based on their genetic makeup and individual response to treatment.

The financial sector is another playground for machine learning innovations. Algorithms rapidly analyze market trends and large datasets to make predictions about stock prices or identify fraudulent activity in real-time. Automated trading systems, powered by machine learning, can execute trades much faster and more accurately than human traders, optimizing investment returns. These systems continually learn from new data, adapting to market shifts and evolving trends, which is crucial in the ever-volatile world of finance.

Within the e-commerce industry, machine learning enhances customer experiences and optimizes operations. Retail giants utilize sophisticated algorithms to predict consumer behavior, recommend products, and manage supply chains efficiently. Personalized shopping experiences have become the norm, with algorithms learning from a user's browsing history and previous purchases to suggest items they are most likely to buy. This not only drives sales but also builds customer loyalty by creating a tailored shopping journey.

The transportation sector is witnessing a revolution fueled by machine learning. Today's public transport systems are becoming smarter with algorithms that predict optimal routes and schedules, reducing wait times for commuters. Perhaps the most groundbreaking application is in the development of autonomous vehicles. Self-driving cars rely on machine learning models to interpret data from sensors, cameras, and other inputs to navigate roads safely. They continuously learn from their environment, improving their driving capabilities over time and promising a future with fewer accidents and increased mobility for people who cannot drive.

Moreover, machine learning is reshaping the entertainment industry. Streaming services like Netflix and Spotify leverage algorithms to curate personalized content libraries for users based on their viewing or listening history. These recommendations systems have drastically changed how we consume media, shifting the power of content discovery from the creators to sophisticated algorithms capable of predicting our tastes.

In agriculture, machine learning facilitates the practice of precision farming, where data-driven insights increase crop yields while minimizing resource use. Farmers use machine learning to analyze weather patterns, soil conditions, and crop health, allowing them to determine the optimal times for planting, watering, and harvesting. This approach leads to more sustainable and productive farming practices, essential as the global population continues to expand.

While applications of machine learning bring a multitude of opportunities, they also raise important ethical and societal questions. The same tools that enhance our lives can also be used in ways that infringe on privacy or lead to biased outcomes, reflecting the biases present in the data they are trained on. As technology continues to advance, it is crucial for industry leaders and policymakers alike to establish frameworks that ensure the ethical deployment of machine learning technologies. Only then can we harness its full potential for the greater good while minimizing its potential risks.

Despite the challenges, the future of machine learning remains bright. As algorithms become more sophisticated and data continues to grow exponentially, machine learning applications will penetrate new domains, solving complex problems that have long eluded human capabilities. From curing diseases to mitigating climate change, the horizon is full of promise for what machine learning can achieve.

In essence, machine learning is not just a tool but a new lens through which we can approach the vast array of challenges and opportunities we face. As it continues to integrate into various aspects of our lives, understanding its capabilities and implications becomes ever more critical. By doing so, we can ensure that this powerful technology is wielded responsibly and inclusively, creating a future that benefits humanity as a whole.

Chapter 20:
Deep Learning Explained

Deep learning, a fascinating subset of machine learning, mimics the human brain's neural networks, enabling machines to identify patterns in vast amounts of data with remarkable accuracy. With layers of artificial neurons, deep learning systems can learn hierarchically—starting from basic features to more complex structures—empowering breakthroughs in fields ranging from computer vision to natural language processing. By harnessing these networks, computers now excel at recognizing speech, translating languages, and even diagnosing diseases with an uncanny precision that was once unimaginable. As deep learning continues to evolve, it's not just carving a path for groundbreaking innovations but also posing profound questions about the nature of intelligence itself and its growing influence on our modern world. This technology's capacity to elucidate hidden insights offers hope for solving some of the world's most pressing challenges, while at the same time, inviting us to ponder its implications for society's future.

Neural Networks and Deep Learning

Deep learning, a subset of machine learning, is revolutionizing the way we interact with technology. At its heart lies a fascinating architecture inspired by the human brain: neural networks. These networks mimic the brain's interconnected neuron systems, empowering machines to recognize patterns, analyze data, and often outperform humans in specific tasks. While the journey from conceptualization to implementation is complex, understanding the fundamental aspects of neural networks lays the groundwork for appreciating deep learning's transformative potential.

A neural network consists of layers of nodes, or "neurons," much like the intricate web of connections in our own brains. These nodes are organized into three vital layers: an input layer, one or more hidden layers, and an output layer. Each neuron in a layer is connected to every neuron in the subsequent layer, allowing information to flow through the network. As data is fed into the input layer, it is processed and transformed by the hidden layers, culminating in the output layer's predictions or classifications.

Training a neural network is akin to teaching a child a new skill. It involves feeding data into the network and comparing its output to the known correct answers. Initially, the network's predictions may be wildly inaccurate. However, through a process called backpropagation, the network adjusts its internal parameters or "weights" to minimize the differences between its predictions and the actual outcomes. This iterative process gradually improves the network's accuracy and performance.

Deep learning is characterized by utilizing networks with many hidden layers, which enable the extraction of intricate features from complex datasets. These features often comprise abstract representations that are crucial for accurate decision-making. For example, in image recognition, early layers might identify basic shapes, while deeper layers learn to recognize complex structures like a cat or a dog.

The staggering advancements in deep learning owe much to the availability of vast amounts of data and significant improvements in computational power. The explosive growth of big data has provided neural networks with the rich datasets required for effective training.

Simultaneously, enhancements in graphical processing units (GPUs) have drastically increased the speed and efficiency of training processes, making deep learning feasible on a much larger scale.

One notable aspect of neural networks is their versatility. Unlike conventional algorithms, which require explicit programming for specific tasks, neural networks learn from examples. This allows them to excel in a wide array of applications, from natural language processing and speech recognition to game playing and autonomous vehicles. As they continue evolving, these systems are blurring the lines between human and artificial cognition.

Despite their power, neural networks come with challenges. One such challenge is interpretability. The decisions made by these networks are often described as "black boxes," meaning it's challenging to discern how they derived a particular conclusion. This lack of transparency can pose significant issues, especially in critical fields like medicine or finance, where understanding the rationale behind a decision is crucial.

Another challenge is the need for large datasets for training. While small datasets can lead to overfitting, where the network performs well on training data but poorly on new data, larger datasets ensure the model learns generalized patterns. Collecting and managing these datasets, however, could raise concerns about privacy and data security, particularly when dealing with sensitive personal information.

Additionally, neural networks consume considerable amounts of computational resources, which may limit their accessibility. The need for substantial hardware investments can be a barrier for smaller organizations or individuals. Fortunately, cloud computing platforms are emerging as a viable solution, offering scalable computing capabilities that can democratize access to deep learning technologies.

The potential of neural networks and deep learning extends into several promising areas for future exploration. Researchers are continuously advancing techniques like transfer learning, where pre-trained networks can be adapted to new but related tasks without extensive retraining. This development holds promise for significantly reducing the computational load and time required to deploy effective models in various contexts.

Moreover, researchers are exploring ways to make neural networks more efficient and environmentally sustainable. Techniques such as pruning, which involves removing unnecessary nodes and connections, and quantization, where models are compressed to use fewer bits for computation, are being explored. These approaches aim to reduce the energy consumption of deep learning systems, making them more ecologically friendly.

In conclusion, neural networks and deep learning are reshaping our world in profound ways. From enhancing everyday technologies to tackling some of humanity's grandest challenges, their influence is undeniable. As we continue to harness their power, fostering a deep understanding of these systems will become increasingly important. Such understanding allows us to leverage their strengths, address their limitations, and critically evaluate the implications of their growing presence in our lives.

Real-World Applications of Deep Learning

Deep learning, a subset of artificial intelligence, is making waves far beyond the realms of laboratories and theoretical pursuits. It's no longer just an academic curiosity; it's an integral part of our lives, touching industries and sectors some of us might never have associated with AI. This transformative technology stands at the intersection of discipline and innovation, bringing forth a new era where machines don't just process data—they learn from it.

In the healthcare industry, deep learning holds immense promise. Diagnosis, traditionally reliant on human expertise and time, has been accelerated by AI. Deep neural networks can analyze medical images with incredible precision, aiding in the rapid identification of conditions like tumors or fractures. Such systems are tireless, analyzing thousands of images without fatigue, and they continue to learn from new data, improving their accuracy with time. AI-powered diagnostic tools are especially critical in underserved regions, providing insights where professionals may be in short supply.

Deep learning is also redefining personal devices and user experiences in ways that seem almost magical. If you've ever interacted with a smartphone assistant, you've encountered deep learning in action. These systems understand and respond to human language, allowing for seamless interaction. They're constantly improving, learning from your commands, and enhancing the user experience, making daily tasks more manageable and efficient.

In the automotive industry, self-driving cars are the epitome of deep learning applications. These vehicles emulate the decision-making of human drivers through layers of neural networks that process data from sensors in real time. They assess speed, detect obstacles, and predict the movements of pedestrians and other vehicles. This level of automation is poised to not only transform transportation but also reduce accidents and enhance mobility for those unable to drive.

Finance is yet another domain experiencing the vast influence of deep learning. Algorithmic trading platforms now analyze market data and execute trades at speeds and efficiency levels that were unthinkable only a few decades ago. Deep learning algorithms also predict market trends, helping investors make better decisions and manage risks more effectively. Fraud detection systems benefit too, using AI to identify suspicious activity by recognizing patterns that indicate fraudulent behavior.

Language translation has evolved dramatically with the introduction of deep learning models. Gone are the days when translation tools would only string words together based on a dictionary lookup. Modern systems can now understand context, humor, and cultural nuances, offering translations that feel more naturally composed and accurate. This has profound implications for global communication, fostering better understanding across languages and cultures.

Creative industries aren't left behind in the deep learning revolution. Artists and musicians are collaborating with AI systems to produce novel art forms and compositions. An AI can compose a symphony, create a painting, or write a story, each reflecting the blend of human creativity and machine intelligence. By experimenting with these tools, creatives expand the boundaries of traditional artistry and open new avenues for expression.

Deep learning also makes its mark in agriculture, where precision farming techniques leverage AI to improve yield. By analyzing data from soil sensors, weather stations, and satellite imagery, AI can recommend optimal planting strategies and monitor crop health. Such techniques not only boost production but also promote sustainable farming practices, conserving resources while maximizing output.

Furthermore, deep learning impacts cybersecurity by fortifying defenses against cyber threats. AI systems analyze potential vulnerabilities and learn from attacks to improve protection mechanisms. These proactive systems can anticipate and neutralize threats before they cause significant damage. The stakes are high, as the safety of personal data and national security often hinge on these capabilities.

In retail, deep learning models analyze customer behavior, enhancing personalization in online shopping experiences. Recommendations systems that suggest products based on browsing history and preferences have become invaluable tools for retailers seeking to engage customers and boost sales. These systems contribute to a personalized shopping experience where each consumer feels uniquely catered to.

Despite its transformative power, deep learning isn't without challenges. It requires vast amounts of data and computational resources, raising concerns around privacy and accessibility. The black-box nature of AI decisions can sometimes be problematic, as the lack of transparency makes it difficult to understand how conclusions are reached. These issues underscore the importance of responsible AI deployment and regulation.

As deep learning technologies continue to evolve, they will further infiltrate aspects of life not yet touched by AI. From improving governmental operations through smart cities to enhancing scientific research methodologies, the potential applications are virtually limitless. As society adapts to these changes, we must consider the ethical implications, ensuring that AI serves the greater good while maintaining transparency and fairness.

The future promises even more sophisticated applications of deep learning, driven by an ever-expanding pool of data and advancements in computational power. Industries will continue to innovate, discovering new ways to integrate AI into processes and products. People will have to adapt to these changes, learning to harness the benefits while managing the risks inherent in such profound technological shifts.

In summary, deep learning is not just a technological feat; it's a catalyst for change, reshaping industries, enhancing human capabilities, and expanding the horizons of what's possible. By exploring these real-world applications, we gain insight not only into current transformations but also into the opportunities and challenges that lie ahead. Embracing deep learning thoughtfully ensures that it remains a force for positive progress in our interconnected world.

Chapter 21:
Human-AI Collaboration

As we stand at the frontier of innovation, the synergy between human ingenuity and artificial intelligence presents a profound opportunity to redefine our world. This collaboration isn't just about enhancing productivity but about evolving our capabilities through a harmonious blend of human intuition and AI precision. By augmenting human strengths with AI-driven insights, we can achieve outcomes previously thought impossible. Whether it's in crafting personalized learning experiences, accelerating scientific discovery, or tailoring healthcare solutions, the partnership between humans and AI holds unparalleled promise. We must cultivate these alliances thoughtfully, ensuring that the human element remains central as AI systems become more pervasive in our everyday lives. In this transformative journey, the success stories scattered across various sectors provide us with a blueprint, reminding us that human creativity, empathy, and ethical stewardship must guide and coexist with AI's computational power. The unfolding narrative of human-AI collaboration reaffirms that together, we can tackle unprecedented challenges and forge a future where technology elevates and empowers our shared human experience.

Enhancing Human Skills with AI

The world is witnessing an unprecedented era where artificial intelligence is making its way into nearly every aspect of human activity. While many fear AI will replace human jobs and capabilities, it's crucial to understand how AI can also complement and enhance human skills, creating synergies that boost productivity, creativity, and problem-solving abilities. In this section, we'll explore the potential AI holds to magnify human capabilities and the promising future of collaborative human-AI interactions.

AI's ability to process enormous amounts of data at speed and scale provides humans with insights and patterns previously unimaginable. For instance, data scientists leverage AI algorithms to sift through complex datasets, revealing trends and insights that guide decision-making. This partnership between data specialists and AI doesn't diminish the scientist's role; instead, it augments their ability to hypothesize and validate results efficiently. By freeing humans from mundane data-processing tasks, AI allows them to focus on strategic thinking and creative problem-solving.

Collaboration with AI tools also empowers employees in industries ranging from finance to healthcare to make more informed and accurate decisions. In finance, for example, AI-driven models can predict market trends based on historical data, which financial analysts then interpret to formulate investment strategies. This synergy leads to more reliable outcomes, combining AI's analytical prowess with the analyst's expert judgment.

Education stands as a significant frontier for enhancing human skills with AI. AI tools revolutionize learning experiences by tailoring educational content to meet individual needs. Adaptive learning platforms use machine learning algorithms to assess student performance in real-time and adjust curricula accordingly. This personalized approach helps students grasp complex concepts at their own pace, ultimately fostering a deeper understanding and retention of knowledge. Teachers, instead of sticking to one-size-fits-all methods, can focus more on providing personalized guidance and mentorship, enriching the educational process.

In creative industries, AI has opened new avenues for expression and innovation. AI-powered platforms can generate art, music, and even literature, providing artists with inspiration and novel ideas. Yet, AI doesn't replace the human touch; rather, it sparks new forms of creativity. Artists harness AI algorithms to explore uncharted aesthetics, blending human emotion and creativity with AI's capability to compute and synthesize vast arrays of possibilities.

In healthcare, AI acts as a powerful ally to medical professionals. Advanced AI diagnostic tools can analyze medical images with extraordinary precision, helping doctors to detect diseases at earlier stages. While AI handles the analysis, healthcare providers focus on the critical aspects of patient care—communication, empathy, and complex decision-making—ensuring that the human element remains at the forefront of medicine.

Industry leaders recognize that training and collaboration are vital in ensuring that employees feel empowered, not threatened, by AI tools. By fostering a culture of learning and adaptation, organizations can facilitate a transformative collaboration between human and machine. Investing in upskilling programs helps workers leverage AI to enhance their productivity and innovation rather than viewing it as a threat.

Moreover, as AI systems become more intuitive, mastering them doesn't necessitate understanding every technical detail. Natural language processing and interface design advancements have made AI tools more accessible, even to those without specialized technical expertise. This democratization of technology ensures that anyone can harness AI's power to improve their daily tasks, making it a universal tool for skill enhancement.

However, the integration of AI to enhance human skills also comes with ethical considerations. There's a fine line between augmentation and dependence. It's crucial for industries to navigate this terrain thoughtfully, ensuring that AI improves capabilities rather than diminishes autonomy or devalues the human workforce.

Ultimately, enhancing human skills with AI signals a more enlightened view of technology—one that sees AI as a partner, not a competitor. By focusing on collaboration, society can usher in a future where technology amplifies human strengths while mitigating weaknesses. This mutual growth fosters not only technological progress but also enriches human experiences, creating a more dynamic, innovative, and inclusive world.

Case Studies of Successful Collaborations

In today's rapidly changing world, the collaboration between humans and artificial intelligence (AI) has become more than just a futuristic concept; it's a reality that's transforming industries and reshaping how we live and work. These partnerships have shown remarkable potential, illuminating pathways where human creativity and intuition join forces with machine efficiency and precision. Let's dive into some of the most noteworthy case studies of successful collaborations that embody the potential of AI and human synergy.

One of the most compelling examples of human-AI collaboration is in the realm of healthcare. The development of advance diagnostic tools like IBM Watson is a prime example. Watson has been employed by hospitals to assist in diagnosing diseases such as cancer. By analyzing vast amounts of patient data, including electronic medical records, clinical trials, and journal articles, Watson can provide potential treatment options that might not be immediately apparent to medical professionals. This doesn't replace the doctor's expertise. Instead, it enhances it by offering insights gleaned from vast swaths of data too cumbersome for any one person to digest.

Another significant area of collaboration is in the creative industries. Consider the world of music where humans and AI are co-composers. OpenAI developed an AI system called MuseNet, capable of generating original compositions in various music styles. By collaborating with human musicians, MuseNet can create pieces that combine the unique emotional expression of human creativity with the complex structural understanding of AI. Artists can begin a song, work it partially with AI input, and then refine it to better convey the intended emotion or message. This collaboration is not about AI replacing composers but serving as a tool that expands creative boundaries.

In architecture and urban planning, AI has been instrumental in solving complex design problems and optimizing the use of space and resources. For instance, Autodesk's AI system, Generative Design, assists architects and engineers in creating thousands of design options based on specified criteria like material costs or environmental impacts. Zaha Hadid Architects, known for their innovative designs, have used these tools to explore and execute avant-garde architectural concepts more efficiently. Human architects input their ideas and constraints, while AI processes these inputs to generate innovative solutions that might not have been initially considered.

The financial sector has also seen fruitful collaborations between humans and AI. In trading floors, AI algorithms analyze market trends and historical data to suggest trades to human traders who then make more informed decisions. This synergy allows traders to react swiftly to market changes, supported by insights from AI systems that predict volatility and price movements. Moreover, AI-powered risk assessment tools enable banks to evaluate loan applications faster and with a nuanced understanding of risk factors, ultimately offering more personalized services to their clients.

Education, too, benefits from human-AI collaboration. AI-driven educational platforms can tailor the learning experience to individual students by analyzing their performance and learning styles. For example, in some classrooms, AI tutors provide personalized feedback and additional exercises where students struggle. Teachers, on the other hand, can focus on providing more one-to-one mentorship and addressing complex student queries. This combined approach works towards creating a more dynamic and individualized learning environment, allowing students to progress at their pace.

Moreover, the agricultural sector has been reaping the benefits of human-AI collaboration through precision farming techniques. AI systems can analyze data collected from drones, sensors, and weather stations to guide farmers on which crops to plant, how to maximize yields, and predict potential threats from pests and diseases. Farms using AI can manage resources more effectively, make informed decisions about crop rotation, and optimize harvest timing. Farmers' expertise, combined with AI analytics, leads to enhanced sustainability and productivity.

Another intriguing example is found in the field of customer service. AI chatbots are used extensively to handle common queries, freeing up human agents to tackle more complex customer issues. Companies like LivePerson have developed AI systems capable of understanding and predicting customer intents. When these systems handle routine inquiries, human representatives can focus their attention on providing personalized experiences and solving unique problems, ultimately improving overall service quality and customer satisfaction.

Finally, let's not overlook the realm of space exploration. NASA's use of AI in developing autonomous rovers is a testament to this collaboration. These rovers, equipped with AI, can navigate and undertake scientific experiments without direct human control, crucial for missions in environments where human intervention is impossible. Scientists program these rovers to accomplish tasks, while AI enables them to respond to unexpected challenges by making real-time decisions based on environmental data. Here, the combination of human ingenuity in designing missions and AI's adaptability ensures the success of far-reaching explorations.

These case studies demonstrate that human-AI collaboration is not just a theoretical ideal but a practical necessity that is shaping the future. The key to successful collaboration lies in leveraging the strengths of both parties: the creative, emotional, and ethical capacities of humans and the analytical, efficient, and scalable capabilities of AI. Together, they can achieve outcomes that neither could accomplish alone, generating innovations that improve industries and enhance the quality of human life.

As we continue to integrate AI into various facets of life, these partnerships will only become more ubiquitous and essential. The future beckons a deeper alliance between humans and machines, and as these case studies show, by embracing this collaboration thoughtfully and ethically, we can unlock incredible possibilities.

Chapter 22:
The Limitations of AI

Artificial Intelligence, for all its wonders, faces significant limitations that reveal its current boundaries both technically and philosophically. Technically, AI systems still grapple with challenges like capturing the nuances of human experience, interpreting contexts beyond pre-set conditions, and generalizing learned experiences to novel situations. Despite advancements, they operate within confined parameters that struggle under the complexity that human cognition handles effortlessly. From an ethical standpoint, AI systems inherit the biases of their creators and datasets, often amplifying societal prejudices. This raises concerns about the fairness and accountability of automated decision-making. Moreover, there are philosophical quandaries about the extent to which AI should mimic human emotion and understanding. As we continue to integrate AI into our world, it's crucial to recognize that while it enhances many facets of life, its limitations remind us that the human mind, with its creativity, empathy, and ethical judgment, remains irreplaceably unique.

The Limitations of AI: Technical Constraints

In the quest to harness the full potential of artificial intelligence, technical constraints invariably stand as formidable challenges. These constraints are the unseen boundaries that delineate what AI can achieve today and hint at the potential future hurdles developers and engineers must contend with. Without understanding these limits, both the optimism surrounding AI and the caution it engenders might be misplaced.

One of the foundational technical challenges is data dependency. AI, particularly machine learning models, rely heavily on vast amounts of data to function effectively. The quality and quantity of this data directly influence the capability of AI systems. Even the most sophisticated algorithms falter when faced with incomplete, biased, or simply insufficient datasets. This dependency raises questions about data accessibility, storage, and the ethical use of data, especially as privacy regulations grow stricter worldwide.

Closely linked to data dependency is the issue of computational limitations. Training complex AI models demands substantial computational power. With the exponential increase in data generation, the demand for processing capabilities also rises. Although advancements in hardware, such as the development of specialized AI chips, are a step in the right direction, they are yet to fully meet the burgeoning requirements. Energy consumption, which accompanies extensive computations, further complicates this constraint, as sustainability goals become increasingly paramount in tech innovation.

Another significant constraint is interpretability, often referred to as the "black box" problem of AI. Advanced AI models, particularly deep learning networks, operate in ways that are not easily interpretable by humans. While these systems can deliver remarkable results, understanding how they arrive at specific conclusions often eludes even the most skilled developers. This opacity poses challenges in fields where accountability and transparency are crucial, such as healthcare and legal systems, potentially hindering wider adoption in these areas.

Beyond the black box problem, there are constraints associated with algorithmic training itself. Many models require extensive training periods and iterative tuning to reach optimal performance levels. This process can be time-consuming and resource-intensive. Moreover, models trained under specific conditions may not generalize well to different environments without significant retraining, limiting their applicability across varied contexts.

Hardware constraints represent another hurdle. While software innovations in AI are rapidly advancing, hardware limitations can impede their implementation. The need for advanced GPUs and specialized processors means that not all individuals or organizations can easily access the required infrastructure to deploy AI solutions. This creates a divide between entities with ample resources and those without, potentially exacerbating existing disparities in AI accessibility and benefit.

The integration of AI systems into real-world applications also unveils challenges related to robustness and reliability. In dynamic and unpredictable environments, AI systems can behave erratically if they encounter scenarios outside their training data. Ensuring that these systems maintain reliable performance in the face of unforeseen disturbances is an ongoing challenge for developers across various industries.

Achieving real-time processing is another critical technical constraint faced by AI. While many applications benefit from rapid AI responses, the latency associated with certain algorithms or the processing power required to achieve them can lead to delays. This is especially problematic in domains like autonomous driving, where timely decision-making is not just ideal, but essential for safety.

Scalability remains a pivotal issue when addressing AI's technical limitations. AI solutions that work well on a small scale often encounter significant hurdles when expanded. Ensuring that AI systems can maintain performance and efficiency as they scale up to meet growing demands continues to be a primary focus for researchers and engineers.

Networking and communication constraints can also affect AI performance. Many AI applications rely on interconnected systems that must communicate efficiently and securely. Latency, bandwidth limitations, and security vulnerabilities in these communications can severely impact the effectiveness and safety of AI deployments, particularly in critical infrastructures like smart grids or connected vehicles.

Despite these constraints, progress continues to be made in mitigating technical challenges through innovation and collaboration across fields. Interdisciplinary approaches, leveraging insights from fields such as neuroscience, cognitive science, and traditional computer science, are increasingly seen as vital in overcoming AI's limitations. By marrying different disciplines, researchers aim to develop more sophisticated models that can learn and adapt in ways analogous to human cognition.

In summary, recognizing and addressing the technical constraints of AI is crucial for unlocking its full potential. These challenges, while daunting, are not insurmountable. They call for creative solutions, continuous research, and collaboration among the global AI community. Embracing these constraints as opportunities for innovation could very well set the stage for the next breakthroughs in artificial intelligence that will redefine the boundaries of what is possible.

Philosophical and Ethical Limits

The realm of artificial intelligence presents us with a myriad of possibilities, offering efficient solutions and transforming industries across the globe. However, as we delve deeper into the AI landscape, we must confront questions that lie beyond mere technical capabilities. These are the philosophical and ethical boundaries that challenge our understanding of AI's role in society, urging us to ponder its implications on human autonomy, moral responsibility, and the essence of thought itself.

At the heart of these philosophical inquiries is the question of consciousness. Can machines, no matter how sophisticated, ever truly "think" or possess consciousness like a human being? While some argue that consciousness remains uniquely human, others posit theories suggesting that emergence of synthetic consciousness is merely a matter of further technological advancement. This debate is more than academic—it raises ethical considerations about the rights and treatments of potentially sentient AI, challenging our traditional views on personhood and morality.

Parallel to questions of consciousness is the ethical challenge of decision-making in AI. As increasingly complex algorithms begin making decisions once left to humans—such as those in medical diagnostics or autonomous vehicles—concerns arise regarding accountability. Who is responsible if an AI system makes a harmful decision? Is it the developer, the user, or the machine itself? The absence of clear ethical guidelines for these scenarios underscores the need for establishing robust frameworks that balance innovation with moral integrity.

Moreover, as AI systems are designed, coded, and trained by humans, they inherently carry the potential for bias. Algorithmic bias can emerge from the data they are fed or the perspectives of those who create them. This can lead to a perpetuation of societal inequalities and perpetuation of stereotypes, raising concerns about justice and fairness. Philosophically, this challenges the notion of AI as an objective tool, highlighting instead its role as a mirror of human imperfections.

Privacy also stands as a major ethical concern in the era of big data and AI. The capacity of AI to analyze and interpret vast amounts of personal data offers unprecedented insights into human behavior, yet it simultaneously threatens individual privacy. The philosophical implications relate to the balance between collective security and personal freedom, urging a reevaluation of privacy rights in an era where data is both omnipresent and valuable.

The philosophical underpinnings of AI extend to existential concerns. As AI systems grow more capable, predictions of a future dominated by superintelligent machines have fueled both anxiety and optimism. Some philosophers speculate about the potential for AI to surpass human intelligence, leading to scenarios where AI determines the fate of humanity. This poses urgent questions about control, safety, and the ethical design of future AI systems to safeguard against unintended consequences.

AI also prompts us to revisit the concept of work and purpose. With predictions that AI could automate many human jobs, there's a philosophical inquiry into the nature of work itself and its role in human fulfillment. If AI handles repetitive and even complex tasks, what becomes of human industriousness? This anticipates a need to redefine meaning and purpose beyond traditional employment, prioritizing creativity, leisure, and social contributions.

Addressing these philosophical and ethical challenges isn't solely about setting boundaries for AI's capabilities. It's about reflecting on what it means to be human and how we choose to integrate technology into our lives. It's about thoughtfully navigating the space where human values intersect with technological possibility, ensuring the benefits of AI are realized without compromising our ethical compass.

In conclusion, the philosophical and ethical limits of AI are as much about the questions we ask as they are about the answers we find. They invite ongoing dialogue and critical reflection, fostering an environment where both innovation and ethics can thrive hand in hand. By engaging with these challenges, we not only shape the future of AI but also illuminate pathways for a harmonious coexistence between intelligent machines and the humanity they aim to serve.

Chapter 23:
AI and Climate Change

The intersection of artificial intelligence and climate change offers a beacon of hope in our battle against environmental degradation. By leveraging AI, we can enhance our ability to model climate patterns, optimize energy consumption, and predict natural disasters with unprecedented precision. AI-driven systems are already revolutionizing the way we manage resources, reducing waste through smart grids, and enabling sustainable agriculture that adapts to shifting weather conditions. However, deploying these technologies at scale presents formidable challenges, including issues of data accessibility, the energy cost of AI itself, and the need for cross-disciplinary collaboration. The potential of AI to drive environmental sustainability is profound, yet it calls for careful consideration of how these technologies are integrated into existing infrastructures and systems, ensuring they contribute positively to the planet's health. The path forward requires us all—governments, corporations, and individuals—to think creatively, act responsibly, and embrace AI's promise as a crucial tool in safeguarding our planet for future generations.

AI Solutions for Environmental Issues

As the effects of climate change become increasingly urgent, the deployment of artificial intelligence (AI) offers promising solutions to tackle environmental challenges. The intersection of AI and climate change is fostering innovative tools that help us better understand, adapt to, and mitigate these issues. This is not just a question of technology but a reimagining of how we can harness AI's capabilities to protect our planet. By analyzing vast amounts of data, AI systems are helping to identify trends, predict outcomes, and create systems that operate more efficiently and sustainably.

One of the most significant contributions of AI is in energy management and efficiency. AI algorithms optimize energy usage by predicting demand and adjusting supply accordingly, ensuring that resources are used efficiently and waste is minimized. In power grids, AI helps balance load and prevent blackouts, while smart algorithms manage the integration of renewable energy sources like wind and solar power, smoothing out variability and improving overall grid reliability. This is particularly important as we shift towards a more renewable-centric energy landscape.

AI is also transforming how we approach conservation efforts. Machine learning algorithms can analyze satellite images to monitor deforestation, track wildlife populations, and detect illegal poaching activities in real-time. These AI-driven conservation efforts give ecologists detailed insights and actionable intelligence, enabling more timely and effective interventions. Additionally, AI is enhancing our ability to protect biodiversity by predicting how species might be impacted by environmental changes and suggesting measures to reduce risks.

Agriculture, a sector both affected by and affecting climate change, is seeing AI-driven solutions that encourage sustainable farming practices. AI systems forecast weather patterns, enabling farmers to adapt to changing conditions and optimize planting schedules. By analyzing soil data, these systems inform decisions about which crops to plant and how to use water resources judiciously, reducing waste and increasing yield. Such precision agriculture techniques not only improve productivity but also minimize the environmental footprint of farming.

Moreover, AI solutions in water management are proving to be invaluable. Sophisticated AI models predict drought conditions and track water usage, allowing for the development of strategies to conserve and distribute water more effectively. Advanced analysis of hydrological data supports planners in creating resilient water systems while also addressing the challenges posed by climate variability. This proactive approach to water management is crucial, considering the growing scarcity and demand for freshwater resources worldwide.

In urban environments, AI promotes sustainable urban development through smart city initiatives. By integrating AI into urban planning, cities can optimize transportation networks and reduce traffic congestion, thus lowering emissions. AI algorithms manage public transit systems in real-time, predicting passenger flow and adjusting services dynamically to enhance efficiency. These technologies contribute to cleaner, more liveable cities by reducing the carbon footprint and improving overall quality of life.

The potential of AI extends beyond direct applications to environmental management and into influencing human behavior. AI-driven platforms can educate individuals and communities about their environmental impact, encouraging actions that contribute to sustainability. For example, personalized recommendations can suggest changes in consumer behavior or energy usage, fostering a culture of sustainability. When AI is used in this way, it acts as an enabler of positive change, motivating people to participate actively in protecting the environment.

However, the success of these AI interventions depends on a collaborative approach between technologists, policymakers, and society. As AI continues to evolve, so does its potential to combat climate change—yet it requires careful consideration of its ethical implications and the distribution of its benefits. Ensuring that AI technologies for environmental issues are accessible to all and leveraged equitably is essential to building a sustainable future for everyone.

Ultimately, while AI presents many powerful tools in the fight against climate change, it is not a panacea. It must be part of a broader strategy that includes policy changes, community engagement, and a commitment to environmental stewardship. With continued development and responsible deployment, AI can significantly contribute to addressing the complex and interwoven challenges that climate change presents. This harmonious collaboration between technology and human effort offers hope for a more sustainable and resilient world.

Challenges in Implementing AI for Sustainability

Artificial Intelligence (AI) holds immense potential for driving sustainable solutions, especially in the context of climate change. However, turning this potential into tangible results is fraught with challenges that need careful consideration. The complexity of AI systems, the massive data requirements, and the integration of AI into existing frameworks are just a few of the obstacles standing in the way. These challenges are not just technical but also involve ethical and socio-economic factors, requiring a multifaceted approach.

One of the primary hurdles is the sheer volume of data needed for effective AI applications. AI thrives on data—the larger and more diverse the dataset, the more accurate and reliable the AI models can become. However, collecting and processing the massive amounts of data required for environmental applications can be resource-intensive and sometimes impractical. This is especially true in regions lacking the infrastructure for data collection and storage, such as remote or underdeveloped areas, where environmental monitoring is often most needed.

Eleanor J. Carter

The intricacies of AI algorithms also pose significant challenges. These systems often act as black boxes, making it difficult to understand how they arrive at specific decisions. In matters of sustainability, where lives and ecosystems may be at stake, the opacity of AI processes can lead to mistrust and resistance. This problem is amplified when AI recommendations contradict traditional ecological knowledge or local sustainable practices, leading to conflicts between tech-driven and community-initiated solutions.

Another significant challenge lies in the integration of AI into existing systems. Many industries related to sustainability, such as agriculture and energy, are deeply entrenched in conventional methodologies. Transitioning these sectors to incorporate AI requires not only technological upgrades but also cultural shifts. Stakeholders must be convinced of AI's value and must adapt to new workflows, which is no small feat in industries resistant to change.

Moreover, AI's resource requirements can sometimes conflict with sustainable goals. The energy consumption of AI models, particularly those using deep learning, is a growing concern. AI training processes can consume vast amounts of electricity, and without sustainable energy sources, this can negate some of the benefits that AI aims to provide. Ensuring that AI development and deployment align with green energy sources is an ongoing challenge that needs innovative solutions and policy interventions.

Ethical considerations further complicate AI's role in sustainability. There is a risk that focusing solely on AI advancements can lead to socio-economic disparities, consolidating power with those who control the technology. Additionally, AI systems can perpetuate existing biases if they're trained on biased datasets, leading to solutions that aren't equitable or just. In climate change mitigation, where the impacts are global yet uneven, ensuring AI fairness and inclusivity is a significant hurdle.

There are also legal and regulatory barriers to consider. AI technology progresses rapidly, often outpacing regulatory frameworks designed to ensure safety and fairness. Safety standards, data privacy, and intellectual property rights must all be addressed in the context of AI for sustainability. Developing regulations that both promote innovation and protect public welfare is a delicate balance that many governments and organizations are still striving to achieve.

Moreover, there is the challenge of interoperability. AI systems are often developed in silos, using different platforms, languages, and standards, which can make integration difficult. Achieving interoperability not only among different AI systems but between AI and existing non AI processes is essential to ensure seamless operation and maximum effectiveness in combating climate change.

Finally, there's the issue of ensuring consistent and adequate funding. AI projects aimed at sustainability can be costly, requiring investments in technology, skilled labor, and infrastructure. While there is increasing interest in green technologies, securing stable, long-term funding is often a challenge, especially when competing with more immediate and perhaps lucrative tech applications unrelated to sustainability.

To overcome these challenges, a collaborative approach is essential. Partnerships between governments, tech companies, researchers, and local communities can help bridge the gap between AI potential and practical implementation. Establishing open standards and promoting transparency in AI systems can foster trust and better integration into existing frameworks.

In conclusion, while AI offers promising pathways to sustainability, the journey is far from straightforward. By addressing these challenges head-on and fostering a cooperative ecosystem, AI can play a critical role in combating climate change and paving the way for a sustainable future. The road may be long and fraught with obstacles, but the pursuit of AI-driven sustainability is a transformative endeavor worth undertaking.

Chapter 24:
Preparing for an AI Future

As we stand on the precipice of a future deeply intertwined with artificial intelligence, the urgency to prepare becomes evident. Our journey forward requires a dual focus on education and policy, aiming to equip both individuals and society as a whole for the challenges and opportunities ahead. Education plays a critical role in promoting AI literacy, ensuring people understand and can critically engage with AI technologies that shape their lives. Meanwhile, forward-thinking policymakers must craft regulations that foster innovation while safeguarding ethical standards and human rights. The coming decades will demand adaptability and foresight, as well as a shared commitment to shaping an inclusive global discourse on AI. By preparing thoughtfully and strategically, we can harness AI's potential to enhance human capability and societal well-being, creating a future that all can navigate with confidence and resilience.

Education and AI Literacy

The landscape of the future is bound to be deeply entwined with artificial intelligence, making education and AI literacy paramount. As our world grows increasingly digital, the ability to understand and interact with AI systems is not just advantageous; it's essential. Educating ourselves and future generations about AI isn't merely about knowing how these systems work; it's about equipping individuals with the tools to thrive in a world where AI shapes nearly every facet of daily life.

The integration of AI into educational curriculums is already underway but remains uneven across different regions and institutions. For some, AI is a subject of intrigue only broached in higher education arenas. Yet, to truly prepare for an AI future, we must cultivate understanding at a much younger age. Imagine a classroom where children learn not only traditional subjects like math and history but also the basics of machine learning and algorithmic thinking. This foundation would encourage critical engagement with AI technologies, transforming students from passive users into informed participants.

However, there's a pervasive challenge: how do we educate about AI when the technology itself is in constant flux? The answer lies in adaptability and fostering a mindset that encourages lifelong learning. Schools and educators should focus less on current technologies and more on the underlying principles of AI. By understanding concepts such as data processing, neural networks, and ethical considerations, students gain a toolkit that remains relevant even as specific technologies evolve.

Beyond educational institutions, AI literacy must permeate society at large. This includes offering accessible resources for different learning levels. Community workshops, free online courses, and public seminars can demystify AI for those who have already left the formal education system. Libraries, community centers, and local governments have a role to play in making AI knowledge available to everyone, helping reduce the digital divide.

AI literacy also involves understanding the broader implications of AI in society. It's crucial to recognize not only what AI can do, but also its potential impacts on privacy, employment, and ethics. Discussions around AI need to be nuanced, encompassing more than just technological capability. Think of it as teaching not just the language of AI programming, but also the societal grammar that dictates its use.

Interestingly, AI itself can assist in its own propagation. AI-driven educational tools can personalize learning experiences, ensuring students understand complex subjects at their own pace. Imagine a virtual assistant that can gauge where a student struggles, providing tailored resources to address specific gaps in knowledge. Such adaptive technologies not only bolster learning outcomes but also model the type of AI students will encounter in the wider world.

Yet, for AI literacy to truly flourish, a concerted effort from various stakeholders is needed. Governments can support AI education through policy and funding, while private sectors can provide insights and expertise. Collaboration can ensure that educational content remains relevant and cutting-edge. This multi-faceted approach could lead to a more AI-literate workforce capable of navigating and contributing to future innovations.

It's important to acknowledge the barriers that exist. Not all schools or countries have equal access to the resources needed to teach AI effectively. This inequality could exacerbate existing educational divides unless steps are taken to make AI learning inclusive and widespread. Philanthropic initiatives and international cooperation could help bridge these gaps, ensuring every child, regardless of geography, has the opportunity to become AI-literate.

As we look towards a future intertwined with AI, consider the implications of failing to adequately prepare the next generation. Without AI literacy, societal divisions could deepen, with a technocratic elite steering decision-making while others remain in the dark. The drive for universal AI literacy is about equity, giving all individuals the power to understand and influence the AI systems that affect their lives.

The journey to widespread AI literacy begins with awareness but grows through action. As individuals, we can seek out resources to improve our understanding. As communities, we can advocate for education systems that emphasize these skills. And as societies, we can prioritize policies that support accessible AI education for everyone.

Ultimately, cultivating AI literacy isn't just about preparing for an AI-driven future; it's about empowering individuals to shape that future. Through education, awareness, and a commitment to inclusivity, we can foster a world where AI enhances human potential rather than limits it. In this way, we ensure that the future—rich in both opportunity and challenge—remains a shared journey, one that we are all equipped to navigate and define.

Policymaking for an AI-Driven World

In an ever-evolving digital age, the influence of artificial intelligence is growing exponentially. As AI continues to integrate deeper into our societal fabric, the role of policymaking becomes critical. It's not just about regulating technology, but about harnessing its benefits while safeguarding against its risks. Policymaking in an AI-driven world demands a delicate balance, requiring foresight, flexibility, and a keen understanding of both technological and human complexities.

To navigate this terrain, policymakers must first ask: What values do we want our AI systems to reflect? This question roots itself in the longstanding ethical debates about technology, but takes on a new urgency with AI's rapid development. Policymakers need to work closely with technologists and ethicists, creating frameworks that emphasize transparency, fairness, and accountability. Embedding these values into AI systems helps ensure they operate in ways that respect human dignity and promote social good.

One of the key challenges in this domain is keeping up with the pace of technological innovation. AI technologies often develop faster than laws can be crafted. This creates a scenario where policymakers are playing catch-up, trying to regulate after technologies have already made significant impacts on society. To address this, proactive and adaptable regulatory approaches are necessary. This could involve more flexible legal structures that can quickly respond to technological advances, or the establishment of dedicated AI oversight bodies that regularly update policies and guidelines as AI evolves.

Moreover, AI policymaking must address the diverse implications of these technologies across different sectors. Education, healthcare, finance, and transportation, to name just a few, all face unique challenges and opportunities when it comes to AI. Policymakers must adopt a sector specific approach, understanding the particular impacts AI could have and crafting policies accordingly. However, they must also recognize that AI doesn't exist in silos; cross-sector policies and interdisciplinary collaborations are crucial for cohesive and comprehensive governance.

In addition, there is the challenge of international consensus. AI is a global phenomenon, transcending borders and affecting nations worldwide. This necessitates international cooperation and dialogue to create consistent standards and practices. Organizations like the United Nations, alongside regional collaborations, can play instrumental roles in facilitating this discourse, helping to harmonize policies and address issues like AI-driven market distortions or labor displacement on a global scale.

For AI policies to be effective, public engagement is equally critical. Policymakers need to involve citizens in the discussion, ensuring their concerns and aspirations are heard. Public trust in AI technologies often hinges on transparency and inclusivity in policy developments. By holding public consultations, educational campaigns, and forums for debate, policymakers can demystify AI for the general populace, making the implications of AI's integration more accessible and understandable.

Furthermore, the responsibility of policymaking extends to ensuring AI literacy. Citizens need to be equipped with the knowledge and skills to engage with AI critically and constructively. This means integrating AI education into public schooling, offering community workshops, and supporting lifelong learning initiatives that keep adults informed of AI's evolving roles. When a society is enabled with AI literacy, it not only becomes more adaptive to technological change but also better prepared for active participation in policy formation.

Finally, policies must also stimulate innovation, not just regulate it. Excessive limitations can stifle creative endeavors and the economic benefits AI can bring. Policymakers should strive to strike a balance, creating a regulatory environment that promotes research and development while ensuring ethical considerations are met. Incentives, grants, and public-private partnerships can stimulate AI innovation, blending technological progress with societal advancements.

In summary, effective AI policymaking is about crafting a future where technology serves humanity. It's about creating systems that protect individual rights and promote societal welfare, and it involves a cooperative effort across sectors, borders, and disciplines. With thoughtful, adaptive, and inclusive policies, we can navigate the complexities of an AI-driven world responsibly and effectively.

Chapter 25:
Empowering Society with AI

In a world increasingly influenced by artificial intelligence, the way societies harness this technology can define our collective future. Empowering society with AI isn't just about technological advancement, but fostering a culture of inclusivity, responsibility, and innovation. Community initiatives are beginning to sprout globally, emphasizing equitable AI access and usage that benefits all layers of society. Encouraging responsible AI use means considering ethical frameworks and implementing policies that ensure AI systems prioritize human welfare and freedom. By fostering collaboration across disciplines and sectors, we can shape AI into a tool not just for efficiency, but for societal transformation—addressing global challenges while enhancing the quality of life. As individuals and communities alike become more AI-literate, they hold the power to guide its evolution, ensuring it becomes a force for empowerment rather than division. It's a societal call to action, where technology serves humanity's best interests and enhances our shared human experiences.

Community Initiatives

In the quest to empower society with AI, community-driven initiatives play a pivotal role. Engaging with AI at the community level isn't just about deploying technology; it's about nurturing a culture of understanding, collaboration, and innovation. These grassroots efforts are central to ensuring that AI benefits everyone, particularly marginalized groups that are often left out of technological advancements.

Many communities have initiated workshops and educational programs to demystify AI concepts. Local libraries, community centers, and schools are evolving into hubs for AI literacy, offering sessions tailored to different age groups and skill levels. Parents and children often participate together, bridging generational gaps and fostering a shared understanding of the digital age. These programs aim to develop critical thinking and analytical skills, equipping people with the tools needed to question and understand AI-driven systems in everyday life.

In addition to educational efforts, community initiatives also include the creation of spaces where citizens can engage in discussions about AI's ethical implications. Forums and town hall meetings allow individuals to voice their concerns, opinions, and hopes regarding AI's role in society. These participatory platforms can drive local policies that reflect community values and priorities, highlighting the importance of democracy in technological adoption.

Moreover, many communities are actively involving themselves in citizen science projects related to AI. By collaborating with universities and tech companies, they contribute to datasets or help develop algorithms that align with community needs. Citizen science not only enriches AI projects with diverse contributions but also democratizes the process of technological innovation, empowering ordinary people to become stakeholders in the scientific community.

Communities are also finding innovative ways to leverage AI to tackle localized problems. For instance, neighborhood associations might use AI tools to monitor and improve air quality or manage waste more efficiently. In rural areas, AI can facilitate agricultural practices, allowing small-scale farmers to optimize their yields with precision techniques that were once accessible only to large enterprises. By customizing AI solutions to fit specific local needs, such initiatives ensure that technological advancements translate into tangible benefits for residents.

Partnerships between tech companies and community organizations are also growing more common, with corporations recognizing the value of engaging directly with the communities they serve. Such collaborations can take the form of sponsorships, knowledge-sharing events, or joint development projects. Through these symbiotic relationships, businesses gain insights into community challenges and aspirations, which in turn informs better product and service design.

However, not all community initiatives are without challenges. There is often a digital divide that needs bridging, requiring not just internet access but also the skills to navigate digital tools. Communities with limited resources may struggle to launch and sustain impactful AI projects. Here, the role of policy and philanthropic bodies becomes crucial. By providing necessary funding and infrastructure, these entities can support community efforts and enhance their capacity to engage with AI meaningfully.

The rise of community initiatives in AI also contributes to the broader movement towards digital equity and inclusion. As communities become more empowered, they can wield greater influence over how AI technologies are developed and implemented. This can drive the agenda towards more ethical and responsible AI practices, aligning technological advances with public good rather than private interests.

Ultimately, community initiatives in AI are about more than just technology—they're about human agency. They represent a collective effort to harness AI not only for economic growth but for social progress. By involving a diverse range of voices and experiences, these efforts ensure that AI serves as a tool for empowerment rather than a source of inequality.

In conclusion, as AI continues to weave itself into the fabric of daily life, community-driven initiatives emerge as vital elements in the tapestry of technological progress. They offer a promising pathway toward a future where AI is not a distant, abstract phenomenon but a familiar and integral aspect of community development and well-being.

Encouraging Responsible AI Use

Our world is increasingly shaped by artificial intelligence, and as it expands its footprint across sectors, the need for responsible AI usage becomes crucial. The power of AI has the potential to transform societies for the better, but without careful consideration, it can lead to unintended consequences. Recognizing responsibility within the AI ecosystem isn't just a mandate for tech giants; it's a shared obligation that communities, policymakers, developers, and users should internalize.

A key starting point in this journey is transparency. When AI systems operate transparently, they foster trust and enable individuals to understand the rationale behind automated decisions. Imagine an AI application in healthcare. If a diagnostic conclusion comes across as a black box with no explanation, it can result in skepticism or rejection by both medical professionals and patients. Demystifying these processes by opening the "black box" allows users to engage in informed discussions about the decisions being made. Transparency empowers individuals to raise questions and seek modifications, consequently helping refine those AI tools.

Equally important is embedding ethical considerations into the design and deployment stages of AI systems. Developers should prioritize creating algorithms that do not reinforce biases or systemic inequalities. In fields like recruitment or law enforcement, for instance, unchecked AI can inadvertently perpetuate societal biases, compounding issues rather than solving them. It becomes imperative to rigorously test AI models against diverse datasets and continually refine them to counteract biases, ensuring equitable outcomes.

Moreover, accountability spans beyond the creation of AI systems to their deployment and use. AI technologies often make critical decisions that affect people's lives, yet determining who is accountable can often be murky. Establishing clear lines of responsibility ensures that when AI errors occur, there are tangible protocols to address and rectify them. Companies should develop robust frameworks to manage these responsibilities, ensuring that there are human oversight and intervention points at all stages of AI operation.

Policymakers also play a pivotal role in encouraging responsible AI use. Legislation can guide the ethical deployment of AI, safeguarding public interest while fostering technological innovation. Collaborative policymaking, in consultation with technology experts, ethicists, and community representatives, can create a balanced approach that addresses the societal impacts of AI. Regulatory bodies can stipulate adherence to privacy laws, data protection guidelines, and set standards for transparency, helping to cultivate an environment where AI can thrive responsibly.

In addition to top-down regulatory measures, grassroots community initiatives can amplify the call for responsible AI. Awareness programs can educate the public about AI's potential and pitfalls, empowering individuals to engage critically with AI tools. This grassroots engagement ensures that the development of AI remains aligned with societal needs and values. Communities can advocate for AI that supports social good, pushing against applications that may benefit a select few at the expense of the many.

Public-private partnerships can further encourage responsible AI use. By combining resources across sectors, these collaborations can foster innovation while keeping ethical considerations front and center. Industry leaders can share best practices and develop guidelines that enable small businesses and startups to implement responsible AI without requiring extensive resources. By establishing standard ethical frameworks and sharing successes and failures, these partnerships set a precedent for the industry.

The education sector holds untapped potential in fostering responsible AI usage. By embedding AI ethics into STEM education and beyond, we equip future generations with the tools needed to question, understand, and challenge AI systems. Learning how to interpret AI's impact across disciplines—be it sociology, economics, or the arts—ensures that a diverse array of voices contribute to the AI narrative. Cultivating AI literacy from an early age enables youths not only to anticipate AI trends but also to influence its trajectory responsibly.

Industry leaders have an opportunity to lead by example, adopting sustainable practices that others can emulate. By volunteering to be stewards of ethical AI use, they can spearhead initiatives that prioritize societal well-being. Conferences, workshops, and hackathons focusing on AI ethics can be opportunities for organizations to showcase their commitment to responsible practices and encourage widespread industry discussion on the subject.

Finally, no discourse on responsible AI use is complete without addressing the importance of public discourse. Encouraging open conversations, fostering civil debates, and inviting diverse perspectives can reveal the blind spots within AI systems. Public forums and interdisciplinary panels can serve as crucibles for innovative solutions, revealing concerns that developers might not have anticipated. By engaging various stakeholders in AI-related dialogues, society becomes an active participant in shaping AI's path.

The potential to reshape society through AI is monumental, and the stakes are undoubtedly high. Yet, by fostering a culture of responsibility that permeates through individual, corporate, and governmental layers, we can ensure AI develops in a manner that justly empowers our societies. Engaging with AI responsibly means acknowledging its profound power, addressing its complexities, and aligning its development with the common good. Embracing this challenge could lead us to an era where AI doesn't merely exist among us, but actively contributes to a just and thriving global community.

Conclusion

As we step back and take a broader view of the landscape painted by artificial intelligence and algorithms, it becomes apparent that we stand on a threshold laden with both promise and uncertainty. AI is relentlessly shaping our world, and it signals that our journey with technology is far from over. This book has sought to illuminate the intricate tapestry woven by AI and algorithms, an endeavor meant to empower and inform, not dictate answers. As our lives become more intertwined with these digital creations, the responsibility to engage critically and compassionately with these systems becomes paramount.

The influence of AI permeates every facet of modern existence—it automates our homes, impacts our work lives, redefines healthcare, and even invades our personal lives through social media. Each of these advancements brings with it questions of ethics, privacy, and control that must be addressed if we are to navigate this new reality responsibly. Awareness and critical engagement are key. By understanding these technologies, we open the door for a world where human and machine coexist beneficially.

Education will undeniably be crucial as we move forward. If we are to live alongside increasingly sophisticated technologies, an informed public capable of interrogating AI systems and their applications is essential. By fostering AI literacy, we can ensure that all individuals, regardless of background, understand how these technologies function and can influence the decisions that impact their lives. Policymakers and educators alike must work tirelessly to incorporate AI education into curricula and public policy.

Moreover, we must continue to cultivate a dialogue around the ethical implications of AI. With immense power comes immense responsibility, and it falls upon society to set the standards for these technologies. Disparities such as the digital divide and bias in algorithmic decision-making must be addressed to prevent AI from exacerbating social inequalities. Meanwhile, embracing international perspectives on AI policy and cooperation could guide us towards a universally beneficial development path.

Despite the challenges, AI offers a myriad of opportunities for innovation and improvement across industries. From precision agriculture that could support sustainable farming practices, to AI-powered innovations in climate change mitigation, the potential for global enhancement is vast. These technologies, when wielded wisely, can drive positive change and foster a more interconnected and resilient global society.

Reflecting on the myriad ways AI has already transformed various sectors, it's crucial to remember that the human element remains central. While AI can augment and sometimes replace human efforts, the creativity, empathy, and moral reasoning unique to humans hold a fundamental role in guiding AI applications. Collaborative efforts, where humans and AI work in tandem, show the promise of amplifying human potential rather than diminishing it.

In this journey, let's not forget the limitations and risks inherent in AI. From technical constraints to philosophical dilemmas about consciousness and autonomy, recognizing where AI falls short can spur innovation and maintain the technology's role as a tool rather than an end. Viewing AI through both its limitations and possibilities enables a balanced perspective, fostering a culture of cautious optimism.

The future alignment of AI with human values will determine its role in society. As AI systems learn and evolve, they should reflect the aspirations of a world committed to fairness, sustainability, and inclusiveness. Our choices today will shape the architects of the future, embedding societal values into digital frameworks that govern our daily interactions.

Ultimately, AI's potential to empower cannot be overstated. It can democratize information, break down barriers of access, and design a future that enhances human well-being on a scale previously unimaginable. Whether through community-driven AI initiatives or institutional efforts to encourage responsible AI use, this is a collective mission. It invites all of us to participate actively and thoughtfully in the creation of a future where AI, like all great tools, serves the greater good.

The narrative doesn't end here. It's an ongoing conversation, a chapter still being written. As algorithms and AI continue to advance, the questions posed become even more vital. The promise and challenges of AI echo the inexhaustible spirit of innovation. Together, guided by understanding and inspired action, we hold the potential to craft a new world that honors both human creativity and technological prowess.

Appendix A:
Appendix

In this appendix, we delve into the supplementary details and additional insights that didn't fit into the chapters but are crucial for a more rounded understanding of artificial intelligence and its far-reaching effects. Here, you might find clarifications on complex concepts, extended discussions on subtle nuances, or data-backed analyses that provide a richer context to the topics touched on throughout the book. From unpacking intricate terminologies to exploring case studies that exemplify the contents of various chapters, this section acts as an invaluable reference point. It's designed to enhance your comprehension and empower you with the knowledge to critically engage with the dynamic, AI-driven world around us. Consider it a bridge connecting you with the vast landscape of innovation, ethics, and societal transformation that AI brings along, cementing the foundational insights needed to navigate the future with confidence and informed curiosity.

Glossary of Terms

Understanding the terms associated with artificial intelligence (AI) and algorithms is crucial for navigating the increasingly complex digital landscape. This glossary provides clear and concise definitions of key terms that frequently appear in discussions about AI and algorithms. Whether you're a tech enthusiast or simply curious about the invisible forces shaping modern life, this glossary is designed to demystify complex concepts and empower you with knowledge.

Algorithm: A set of rules or instructions given to a computer to help it perform a specific task. Algorithms are used in a wide range of applications, from simple calculations to complex data processing in AI systems.

Artificial Intelligence (AI): The simulation of human intelligence processes by machines, especially computer systems. These processes include learning, reasoning, and self-correction.

Big Data: Extremely large data sets that may be analyzed computationally to reveal patterns, trends, and associations, especially relating to human behavior and interactions.

Deep Learning: A subset of machine learning involving neural networks with many layers, which enable learning from data representations rather than task-specific algorithms.

Machine Learning: A method of data analysis that automates analytical model building. It is a branch of AI based on the idea that systems can learn from data, identify patterns, and make decisions with minimal human intervention.

Neural Network: A series of algorithms that mimic the operations of a human brain to recognize relationships between vast amounts of data. These networks form the basis of deep learning.

Autonomous Vehicle: A vehicle capable of sensing its environment and operating without human involvement. Autonomous vehicles use various technologies such as AI, sensors, and GPS to navigate and communicate.

Ethics of AI: Concerns the moral implications and decisions involved in the development and usage of AI technologies, including issues of privacy, bias, and decision-making authority.

Data Privacy: The aspect of data protection that focuses on handling data properly (compliance with data protection and privacy laws). It often involves ensuring that data is collected, processed, and stored in a manner that protects individual privacy rights.

AI Literacy: The ability to understand and engage with AI technologies, recognizing their potentials and limitations, and critically assessing their impact on society.

Surveillance: Monitoring of behavior and activities through the use of technology, often for the purpose of influencing, managing, or directing. AI has advanced surveillance capabilities dramatically, raising both opportunities and ethical concerns.

Automation: The technology by which a process or procedure is performed with minimal human assistance. Automation is pivotal in increasing efficiency and productivity across various industries.

This glossary serves as a foundation for understanding the complex narratives surrounding AI and algorithms. By familiarizing yourself with these terms, you'll be better equipped to participate in discussions, make informed decisions, and appreciate the innovations that are reshaping our world.

Resources for Further Reading

To truly grasp the depth and breadth of artificial intelligence and algorithms, exploring additional resources can be invaluable. While the main chapters in this book provide a comprehensive overview, diving into specialized materials can deepen your understanding and appreciation of the field. From books and academic articles to online courses and lectures, a myriad of resources is available to satisfy your curiosity and answer any lingering questions.

Books are a traditional yet reliable source of knowledge. For those seeking a more detailed historical context, "Machines of Loving Grace" by John Markoff explores how human and machine coexistence has evolved over time. Meanwhile, Nick Bostrom's "Superintelligence: Paths, Dangers, Strategies" provides an insightful look into the future possibilities of AI and the potential risks involved. To understand the ethical implications, you might consider Cathy O'Neil's "Weapons of Math Destruction," which delves into how big data and algorithms can sometimes reinforce inequality and threaten democracy.

Academic journals offer a plethora of peer-reviewed articles that address cutting-edge research and ongoing debates in the AI and algorithms space. Journals like *Artificial Intelligence Journal* or *Machine Learning Journal* often publish studies that push the boundaries of what's currently possible. These publications can provide a more technical perspective, ideal for readers who wish to delve into specific challenges or innovations within the field.

If you prefer a more interactive approach, numerous online courses can guide you through the complexities of AI and algorithms. Platforms like Coursera, edX, and Udacity offer courses from reputed universities. Andrew Ng's Machine Learning course, a staple in AI education, is hosted on Coursera and has been instrumental in introducing the basic concepts to a wide audience. For more hands-on experience, Udacity's "Intro to Artificial Intelligence" nanodegree offers practical projects that build foundational knowledge.

Documentaries and lectures available online provide another engaging way to learn about AI. TED Talks often feature discussions by leaders in the field, offering perspectives that blend technological insight with societal implications. For instance, lectures on how algorithms affect privacy and decision-making can provide a quick yet deep dive into specific topics. Various streaming services also host documentaries focused on the influence and impact of AI in both mundane and extraordinary domains.

AI-centric organizations and think tanks often produce reports and white papers that are both informative and forward-looking. The Partnership on AI and the Institute for Ethical AI and Machine Learning publish guidelines and policy papers that aim to foster transparency and accountability in AI technologies. Reading these materials can keep you abreast of the ethical standards being developed in real-time.

Community forums and discussion boards like Reddit's Machine Learning community or the AI Stack Exchange offer platforms for enthusiasts and experts alike to discuss recent trends, troubleshoot issues, or simply share knowledge. These communities are invaluable for anyone looking to engage in conversations and gain diverse insights about how algorithms operate and impact our lives.

Finally, keeping up with news from dedicated tech outlets such as Ars Technica, TechCrunch, and Wired can ensure you're aware of the latest developments. These sources offer news about breakthroughs, challenges, and the ever-evolving role of AI in society. Regularly reading such content can help you understand the dynamism of the field and its various intersections with everyday life.

As you explore these resources, remember that AI and algorithms are not just subjects of scientific inquiry but are deeply interwoven with cultural, ethical, and political dimensions. Engaging with a broad range of materials will provide you with a holistic understanding, enabling you to critically and thoughtfully participate in ongoing discussions about the role of AI in our world.

www.ingramcontent.com/pod-product-compliance
Lightning Source LLC
Chambersburg PA
CBHW051239050326
40689CB00007B/987